THE LAST BET

One Man's $150,000 Education in Modern Sports Betting

Julian Harlow

This is a work of nonfiction. Some names and identifying details have been changed to protect the privacy of individuals.

First Edition

ISBN: 979-8-9957282-0-7

Disclaimer

This book is for informational and educational purposes only and does not constitute medical, psychological, or financial advice. The author is not a licensed medical, mental health, or financial professional.

The content is based on personal experience, publicly available data, and general research. While every effort has been made to ensure accuracy, no guarantees are made regarding the completeness or reliability of the information presented.

Any actions taken based on the contents of this book are done at the reader's own risk. The author is not responsible for any outcomes resulting from the use or misuse of the information provided.

If you are experiencing issues related to gambling, addiction, or mental health, seek help from a qualified professional or a recognized support organization.

Contents

Prologue

The man at the craps table didn't look like he had $40 million. He looked like a guy who'd just gotten off shift somewhere — stocky, mid-fifties, Greek, the sort of build you get from a lifetime of being on your feet. No entourage. No jewelry, no swagger. He wasn't performing. He was just there, every night, at the Binion's Horseshoe in downtown Las Vegas, throwing dice while the chips piled up in stacks the casino staff had stopped trying to count casually.

His name was Archie Karas. Three years before this, he had walked into Vegas with $50.

Not a typo. Fifty dollars. He had driven in from Los Angeles, where he'd been working as a waiter and playing poker in underground games, and where a bad run had taken pretty much everything he had. So he borrowed $10,000 from a friend, sat down at a poker table, and within a few weeks had turned that into a million dollars by beating the best players in town one by one. After a while nobody would sit across from him anymore.

So he switched to pool. Same outcome. He started staking his own opponents, handing them the money they were going to bet against him, just to keep the action going, and even that dried up. Then he found craps, and for two years the dice did the same thing the cards and the cues had done. He ran the bankroll from a million up to forty. The longest, largest documented winning streak in Vegas history. The casinos raised their table limits to keep him playing.

Other gamblers stopped playing entirely and stood around watching him roll. The whole city knew his name.

He lost it all in three weeks.

Not gradually, not through some long slow erosion. He sat down at the same tables and the streak ended, and he kept betting because that's what your brain tells you to do after two years of winning — keep going, the edge is still there, the next roll has to be the one. It wasn't. None of them were. He walked out of Vegas with a thousand dollars in his pocket, basically the same broke-and-starting-over he'd been when he arrived, except this time he had spent two years sitting on top of forty million and watched it disappear in less than a month.

When most people hear that story, the first instinct is the same one I had: he must have panicked. He must have lost it. He must have done something dumb that he wouldn't have done at thirty million. He didn't. He did exactly what his brain told him to do, which was the exact same thing his brain had been telling him to do for the previous two years; the only thing that changed was the dice. Same instinct that built the forty million destroyed it, not a flaw in his character. A feature of how a human being processes winning.

I thought about Archie a lot during the week I lost a hundred and fifty thousand dollars, not because our situations were the same. They weren't, not even close, but because the mental math underneath them was identical.

By 2025 I'd been betting for four years, not casually. Millions of dollars wagered across four full seasons of wins and losses and resets. I'd had the big years; 2024 alone ended well into six figures, capped by a $124,000 parlay hit that felt less like luck and more like proof I'd figured something out. I'd had the hard years too — 2022 and 2023, where I'd run a balance up to twenty or thirty thousand and then watch it evaporate over a single weekend, then rebuild it over a few months and do the whole thing again. Every time the cycle completed, I came out of it with one more piece of evidence that I could survive it. That I was different. That I knew when to push and when to pull.

There were people around me who saw what was coming before I did. I wasn't ready to hear them.

I had a track record. I had evidence. I was the guy in my circle who actually came out ahead, and that identity had become as real to me as anything else I'd built. So when the losses started coming that week in 2025, I didn't panic; I did what felt completely rational, which was to keep going. I was Archie at the dice table. Just at a different scale, on a phone instead of a casino floor.

The number is different. The story is the same.

The name on this cover isn't my real one. Julian Harlow is the version of me that can speak freely. I picked it because what I'm about to say matters more than who's saying it, and my real life is loud enough as it is. I've made money and lost it. I've led companies, sat in boardrooms, shaken hands with people who quietly run entire industries. I've been flown out and put up and kept close by people whose actual job is making sure men like me stay plugged in.

None of that protected me, not from the truth, and not from the systems built to consume us.

If you're under thirty-five there is, statistically, a betting app on your phone right now or there has been one in the last twelve months. Maybe you downloaded it once just to try it. Maybe you use it the same way you order a ride or stream a show. Legislation and tech have put casinos into the spaces you already live in, and that's not me being dramatic — that's the actual stated business model. The betting industry wants to be wherever you are, woven into your day, indistinguishable from the other apps you barely think about anymore.

What happened to me wasn't a fluke. It wasn't some spectacular miscalculation by a guy who didn't know better. It was the predictable result of conditions shaped by technology, marketing, design, and basic human biology. I had read the psychology. I had training in emotional intelligence. I had business sense, and an exit, and resources, and people around me who would have helped if I'd asked.

None of it insulated me. If somebody who understands the mechanism can still get taken, then the mechanism is powerful. And if I can get misled by it, so can you.

I chose clarity over vanity writing this. I'm going to name systems, explain methods, show calculations, and tell stories — personal ones that connect the math to actual human consequences. I want you to read a number and feel what it does to a life. I want you to understand both how the industry works and how your own brain reacts to it.

I'm not going to lecture you. I don't think willpower is the answer to anything, and I'm not going to write a book pretending it is. What I'm trying to do is explain how this stuff actually works and give you something useful to do with that information. I'll be direct because direct is what I needed when I was in it. If this book changes one mind, gets one family to have a hard conversation they would have skipped otherwise, helps one person see a pattern early enough to step out of it, I'll consider it worth the time it took to write.

Twenty years ago, if you had a gambling problem, you went to places you could avoid. Casinos. Racetracks. A guy named Vinny in the back of a deli somewhere. Those places had friction built in, you had to want it badly enough to physically go and get it, and you had to settle up with a person on the other side. Today that friction is gone. Your phone is built to keep your attention, and the same playbook the platforms use to keep you scrolling is the playbook the apps use to take your money. They send you a notification when you're bored, when you're between meetings, when you're up late on a Sunday. They mine the quiet moments in your day. They are not selling you sports. They are selling you a relationship with them, and they're designing that relationship to be hard to put down.

Archie Karas had to walk into a casino to lose $40 million.

All I needed was my phone.

PART ONE

THE RUN

Everyone has a reason they're different.

CHAPTER 1

The First Bet

I was twenty years old the first time I had real money and no idea what to do with it.

I'd just crossed six figures for the first time, not a salary, money I'd made myself, the kind that feels almost fake the first time you see it because nobody in your family had ever prepared you for what that number actually looks like sitting in your account. I was living in Las Vegas, traveling constantly, spending freely, moving through the world with the particular confidence of a kid who'd figured something out early and hadn't yet learned what the bill was going to look like.

That fall a few of my friends were headed to Tucson for a weekend. People from different parts of my life were converging at U of A, staying at a frat house, the kind of loosely organized trip that happens when everyone is twenty-something and nobody has anywhere they actually need to be. I drove out to meet them.

It was dusk when I got there. That very specific desert dusk where the sky goes orange and pink before it goes dark, the air still warm enough that you forget it's October, the campus loud with people who also had nowhere to be. We were at someone's place. Drinks going. A weekend that hadn't decided what it was going to be yet.

One of the guys pulled me aside at some point during the night. He had a friend who ran a book. Could get me in if I wanted. Low friction, just needed a reference; his guy was solid.

I said sure. Why not.

The first week I won. I don't remember the exact amount but it was enough to feel like confirmation, like I'd found something that worked, like the money I was already making had a new place to go and grow. Second week I lost some of it back. Paid him. That felt fine, normal, part of the game.

Then came the big loss. I don't even remember what game it was. I remember the number — about five thousand dollars that I now owed to a man I had never met, connected to me through a chain of friends and introductions, no contract, no court, no formal anything. Just an unspoken understanding: you pay what you owe.

I didn't pay.

I told myself I'd handle it eventually; I'd figure something out. That it wasn't a real debt the way other debts are real. What I actually did was ghost him. Stopped answering the number. Stopped responding to messages. Disappeared into the ordinary business of my life and hoped the problem would get tired of me.

It didn't get tired of me. It called.

For seven months his people kept reaching out. Calls and texts. Nothing violent, nothing cinematic, just relentless and annoying. That low-grade, in-the-background stress of an unpaid debt you keep ignoring because the alternative is admitting you owe someone something. I'd see the number light up and know what it was before I even looked. It wasn't fear, exactly. More like a recurring inconvenience I hadn't figured out how to end.

I don't know what finally made me respond. Maybe I just got tired of it. Whatever the reason, I sent him a message one day, genuine and direct, acknowledging the debt and proposing something that in retrospect tells you everything about where my head was.

I didn't want to just hand over the money. So I offered him a bet.

He picks the game. I put the $5,000 on whatever he chooses. If it hits, he gets his money and I keep the winnings; if it loses, I pay him the debt and we're done. Either way it ends.

He agreed.

I sent the money to a friend in Las Vegas, a different friend, someone with no idea any of this was going on, no knowledge of the bookie or the debt or the seven months of calls. Just a guy I trusted who happened to be near a casino sportsbook. I told him I needed a bet placed. He texted me a photo from inside the book — him at the window, saying he was putting it in now. I forwarded the screenshot to the bookie. *Bet being placed. Fingers crossed.*

I was at a bar when the game ended. Checked my phone. The bet had lost.

I waited to hear back.

Nothing. The bookie just went quiet. Calls stopped, texts stopped, the whole thing evaporated like it had never happened. I never heard from him again.

Later that day my friend sent the money back. The line had been too long, he said. He couldn't get the bet in before the game started. He'd just held onto it.

I was pumped. I'd just gotten $5,000 back that I'd already written off as gone, and my friend had no idea he'd accidentally resolved the entire situation, to him he was just returning money from a bet that hadn't gotten placed. He had no clue about any of it.

I didn't bet again after that, not because I was scared or scarred by the experience; the bookie was more annoying than anything else, just relentless with the calls. The whole thing had enough friction attached to it that walking away felt easy. Real person. Real pressure. Real debt that required real resolution.

I didn't miss it. I didn't think about it. That was the end of it.

For two years.

I was twenty-two when it came back, and it came back differently.

It was a Sunday afternoon in Scottsdale. I was sitting at a bar with four other guys, watching NFL games on screens I couldn't quite reach from where I was sitting. Business was good; better than good. My company had crossed six million in revenue that year. I had the kind of easy confidence that comes when things are going right and you don't yet know what going wrong feels like.

During halftime, one of the guys at the table pulled out his phone and started laughing at something on the screen.

"What?" someone asked.

He turned it around. His betting app. He'd hit a parlay the week before — something like a thousand off a hundred-dollar bet. The ticket was still pulled up, all green checkmarks down the page. He scrolled through it like a guy showing off his stock portfolio.

"You're not on yet?" he asked me.

I wasn't. He pulled up the app, entered a referral code, and handed me my phone back. I had free play money already loaded before I'd actually agreed to anything. Three minutes start to finish. No bookie. No introduction. No obligation to anyone. Just an account with someone else's money in it, sitting there waiting for me to do something with it.

I put fifty dollars on an NFL parlay. Four teams, all favorites I felt good about. It felt like daily fantasy, which I'd done casually before. Same energy, same category.

All four covered. I won a little over three hundred dollars.

That first win didn't feel like money. It felt like a signal. Like I'd found a new channel — not just for making money but for being part of something my friends were already in on. It felt modern. Like I'd unlocked a feature I hadn't known existed.

Here's the difference between twenty and twenty-two. At twenty, betting required something from you. A connection. A person. A relationship that came with real obligations and real consequences when you didn't honor them. The bookie wasn't an app; he was a guy, connected to other guys, who knew how to find you and wasn't going to stop calling until things got settled. That friction was annoying and at times genuinely inconvenient, but it was also protective in a way I didn't fully appreciate until it was gone.

At twenty-two none of that existed anymore. A referral code. Free play money. No person on the other end who could call you for seven months. Just a phone and an account and a balance that went up or down with no real-world consequence attached to either direction except the number itself.

That shift, from friction to frictionless, is the whole story of what happened to my generation and gambling. The old model required you to want it badly enough to seek it out and accept the terms that came with it. The new model handed you free money to get started and made the whole thing feel like a feature you'd been missing.

I walked out of that Scottsdale bar three hundred dollars up and completely certain that I'd figured something out.

It would take four more years to find out what I'd actually done.

Gambling is older than most empires. Long before markets and kings and anything we'd recognize as a country, people were already making bets, shells, bones, carved stones, simple promises between two guys who wanted something to ride on. Those early wagers weren't really about money; they were social. They marked celebrations, settled disputes, created stories that lasted longer than the night they happened on. The reason that history matters is because it shows you something most modern coverage of gambling skips: the pull toward risk isn't a glitch or a defect. It's part of how we're built. Which is also why fighting it with willpower alone tends not to work.

What's new isn't the urge. What's new is how fast that urge can become a habit, and how easily you can lose everything before you even notice what's happening.

The moment that made all of this possible came in 2018. The Supreme Court ruled in *Murphy v. NCAA* and struck down the federal law that had kept most states from authorizing sports betting. What had been niche and underground became legitimate almost overnight. Capital came pouring in. Apps got built. Companies that had been operating in the shadows suddenly had a legal runway and went after the entire country at once.

The result was that places you used to have to visit became things that came to find you.

Early wins aren't accidents, they're strategy. A first win rewires something in your head; the brain tags the action as significant, files it away, starts looking for ways to repeat it. Escalation happens gradually. Small losses grow as your confidence does. At some point an algorithm somewhere notices you're high-volume and suddenly there's a person texting you. Offers with your name on them. Access that makes you feel like you've earned a seat at a different table.

That's when transactions start to feel like a relationship. And that's where the real damage starts.

The products themselves are designed to push you toward whatever's worst for you. Parlays are the clearest example — small stake, big payout, the interface makes them look like a smart play. The math tells a completely different story, and I'll show you exactly what that looks like in the next chapter.

Beyond parlays, live betting turns every single minute of a game into a decision. Micro-bets let you wager on individual plays. The whole interface is built to keep the window between impulse and action as small as possible. Because the smaller that window is, the less time your rational brain has to intervene.

I knew none of that sitting in Scottsdale at twenty-two, walking out three hundred dollars up with a feeling I couldn't quite name but already wanted to feel again.

I'd been here before. I just didn't recognize it yet as the same place.

CHAPTER 2

The Machine

When people say the house always wins, they usually mean it as a shrug. Something you say to close the conversation. And the shrug is right. It's just incomplete.

The house doesn't win because of luck. The house wins because the rules are written so that winning long-term is basically impossible for the person on the other side of them. That isn't an accident; it's the whole business model.

Sports betting isn't a side market anymore. It's massive, and it's growing fast. The global sports betting market sat around $100 billion in 2024. The wider gambling industry is in the hundreds of billions and on track to push close to a trillion dollars within this decade. In the U.S. Alone, sports betting revenue hit record numbers after the 2018 Supreme Court ruling opened the floodgates state by state, well into the double-digit billions, and climbing every year.

Those numbers exist because of three things working together: the juice, the product design, and the loyalty machine. Understand all three and you understand exactly why the math always catches up — no matter who you are, no matter how sharp you think you are.

The juice is the simplest one, and it's the one most people never notice because it's built directly into the odds.

Here's how it works. Two teams are evenly matched, a genuine fifty-fifty shot either way. A fair payout would double your money if you win. But the books don't offer that. Instead of paying $2.00 for every $1 you bet, they pay $1.90. That ten cents per dollar is their cut, the juice, or "the vig" if you want the older term that the older guys still use.

Picture it at scale. A thousand people put $1 on each side of a coin flip. The book collects $2,000. It pays back $1,900 to whoever happens to land on the right side. It keeps $100 for doing nothing except setting the line and processing the bets.

That isn't cheating. That's just how the market is structured. But multiply that margin across millions of transactions every week and you start to understand why this industry pulls billions in revenue without ever needing a single bettor to lose dramatically. They just need everyone to keep playing.

The product that extracts the most from bettors is the parlay, and it's worth taking a minute on the math; not because the math is complicated, but because the gap between how it feels and what it actually does is where most people get quietly destroyed.

A parlay combines multiple bets into one ticket. The pitch is simple: small stake, huge potential payout. Put $10 on six games and win a thousand. The app makes it look exciting; the interface highlights the multiplier; you think you're being smart, using your knowledge across multiple games, stretching your money efficiently.

Here's what's actually happening.

You build a six-leg parlay and put $100 on it. The average bettor wins roughly half their individual picks, so 50% per leg is realistic. Each leg you add cuts your odds in half. By the time you get to six legs, you're sitting at about a 1.5% chance of winning. Translation: out of every hundred times someone builds that ticket, it hits once or twice.

A six-leg parlay typically pays around 45 to 1, so your $100 returns $4,500 if it lands.

Now the math.

Out of every hundred people who placed that same bet, 98 of them lost $100. Two of them won $4,500. The book collected $9,800 from the losers and paid out roughly $9,000 to the winners. They kept $800 for doing nothing except building the app.

That's the parlay. It isn't a long shot that occasionally pays off — it's a product engineered so the house always keeps a cut no matter what, and the longer you keep building tickets, the more certain that math becomes.

Parlays aren't a bug in the system. They're the system's best product. The apps push them hardest because the margins are enormous. Every "parlay boost" notification, every "same-game parlay" prompt, every interface feature that makes it easy to add one more leg — all of it exists because parlays are the highest-margin bet on the menu, and the house knows it even when you don't.

I built hundreds of parlays convinced I was being strategic. The math didn't care.

Live betting is the parlay's evil twin. Same dynamic, high house edge, easy to escalate, but with time pressure layered on top. The platform prices events in real time. Every play is a new line. Every momentum shift is a new opportunity. The whole interface is engineered to keep you engaged minute by minute, decision by decision, and that immediacy is exactly the point. When you're reacting in real time, the window between impulse and action gets so small that your rational brain barely gets a word in.

I'd watch a first quarter go sideways and feel the pull immediately. The team I'd bet wasn't covering. The live line was right there. One adjustment and I could fix it. What I was actually doing was making a financial decision in roughly the same mental state as someone swerving to avoid a car on the highway. The platform was designed for that state. I wasn't.

The acquisition and retention machine is the third piece, and it's the one that gets personal.

Getting a new high-volume bettor costs the company real money — sometimes hundreds of dollars in promotions and incentives per person. So once you're in and betting at real volume, the company does everything it can to keep you there. Deposit bonuses. Matched bets. Loyalty points. Push notifications timed to moments of boredom or stress. And for the bettors flagging as genuinely high-value, something more personal than any algorithm.

It was 2024, a few days before Thanksgiving. I was in Las Vegas, and I had spent that day doing something that had nothing to do with gambling. I'd bought $15,000 worth of food from Costco. Turkeys, sides, the whole thing, to donate as Thanksgiving meals for families that needed them. Ten or fifteen people had shown up with trucks. We spent the entire day loading vehicles, coordinating drop-offs, getting it out into the city. The kind of day that leaves you tired in a good way.

I got home and my phone buzzed. Unknown number.

Hey, this is Mike. I'm your VIP host. Just wanted to introduce myself; if you ever need anything at all, don't hesitate to reach out.

I hadn't asked for a VIP host. I didn't even know that was a thing that existed. I remember reading the text and thinking it was almost quaint, the way you might react to getting a card in the mail from your bank. I didn't reply right away.

Mike was patient. Over the next few days he kept reaching out. March Madness tickets. Golden Knights games. Suite access for NFL Sundays. He'd text the way a friend might — *hey, got some great seats for Thursday if you're around*, always low-pressure, always generous, always perfectly timed.

What I didn't know yet was what had triggered that first text. I had wagered over $50,000 in a short window. Their system had flagged me. Mike's actual job; his entire job — was to keep me betting. The tickets weren't perks; they were investments with an expected return. Every suite, every game, every casual text was a calculated move to deepen a relationship that would, over time, make walking away feel wrong.

There's a term for this in behavioral economics: the sunk cost of social capital. Once someone has done you enough favors, leaving starts to feel like betrayal. You aren't just closing an app. You're walking away from Mike, who got you those seats, who always texts back, who treats you like you matter.

By the time I understood what was actually happening, it had already worked.

The industry isn't creating value. It's moving money from bettors to shareholders, one relationship at a time. The gross gaming revenue you hear about in industry reports — that's just the gap between what bettors wagered and what they got back. Every dollar in that number came out of someone's account.

They also use intermittent reinforcement, which is the same mechanism that makes slot machines so effective and social media so hard to put down. Wins that arrive randomly and unpredictably are more addictive than wins that arrive on a schedule, because the unpredictability keeps the brain searching for the pattern. A win streak makes you feel like you've cracked something. A losing streak makes you feel like you're one good bet away from fixing it. The platform is designed to keep you cycling between those two states for as long as possible.

None of this is hidden, by the way. The industry publishes its revenue. The product design is visible to anyone who's paying attention.

The problem is that nobody is paying attention to the mechanics when they're watching the game. And the people who built these products know exactly which moments those are.

That isn't an accident either.

CHAPTER 3

THE CHASE

I want you to picture something. Not a betting slip or a casino floor, just the feeling inside your chest when a bet hits. That sudden lift. The release. The little explosion of relief and satisfaction that fires off before you've even fully processed what happened.

That moment is real. It's chemical. And your brain files it away immediately, because that's what brains do; they track what felt good and start looking for ways to repeat it.

That's dopamine doing its job. Dopamine isn't actually a reward, it's a learning signal. It marks certain actions as important and tells your brain to remember them. In a survival context it helped our ancestors remember where they had found food. In a modern context it helps you remember exactly how it felt when that parlay hit. The problem is that betting apps are specifically engineered to trigger that response over and over, concentrated and fast and relentless. Your brain doesn't know the difference between finding food and hitting a four-leg parlay at midnight. It just knows something good happened, and it wants to do it again.

When you win, the brain encodes the whole situation, not just the money. It records the context. What you were wearing, where you were sitting, who you were with, what you were feeling. A small unexpected win late at night, when you're bored and half-scrolling, can land disproportionately hard because there's nothing competing with it for your attention. Add a friend texting *let's go* and that memory gets even stickier. The win starts to feel like proof — that you're sharp, that you read the game right, that you actually know what you're doing.

That memory is what the industry is selling you.

I felt it most clearly the week I got back from Peru. I'd been gone for a stretch. Walked through parts of the Amazon, spent time in the forest, the kind of trip that disconnects you from everything familiar. No routines, no screens, no notifications, just the river and the noise of the jungle and the feeling of being somewhere completely outside your normal life. I came back jet-lagged and wired in equal measure; that specific energy you get when you've been unplugged for a while and suddenly the whole world is available to you again.

First night back I put $10,000 on Thursday Night Football. It doubled. Just like that.

That win didn't feel random. It felt like the natural continuation of a good stretch, like the universe had been quietly saving something up for me while I was gone and was now paying it out. That isn't rational. I know it isn't. But that's exactly how it felt, and that feeling is the whole mechanism.

Saturday morning I threw the entire $20,000 on a college football game. It hit. I didn't wait — I rolled $25,000 onto an afternoon game. When that one cleared, I was sitting at $70,000. Everything felt locked in. I was flowing. Every pick felt inevitable rather than like a guess.

By Sunday, after two more bets on NFL games, I was at $130,000.

I remember staring at that balance and thinking about what I'd do with it. A down payment on an investment property. Something real, something that would still be there in a year. The thought to cash out crossed my mind more than once. I chose not to.

The following Thursday I lost $20,000 in a single game.

I was at a friend's house. Nobody knew how much I had on it. I just got quieter as the game went on. When it ended I felt devastated, but there was something else underneath the devastation too, a certainty that arrived before I'd even fully processed the loss.

I have to win it back.

There's a reason that thought feels so urgent. Daniel Kahneman and Amos Tversky's research on *loss aversion*; the foundational work that earned Kahneman a Nobel Prize in 2002 — shows that losses register in the human brain at roughly twice the emotional intensity of equivalent gains. A $20,000 loss doesn't feel like a $20,000 gain in reverse; it feels closer to a $40,000 hit. That asymmetry is what makes the chase feel rational in the moment. Recovering the loss isn't framed as winning new money; it's framed as restoring something that was taken. The brain treats the recovery as a higher-priority goal than ordinary winning, and it will tolerate worse odds and bigger bets to get there. I wasn't gambling when I bet to win it back. From my brain's perspective, I was correcting an injustice.

That instinct is worth understanding because it feels completely rational in the moment. The brain wants to fix mistakes. Recovering a loss doesn't feel the same as winning something new — it feels like justice. Like restoring something that was taken from you. Like you're owed it. And because it feels like justice rather than gambling, you don't apply the same skepticism you'd otherwise bring to a bet. You aren't chasing a win. You're correcting a wrong.

That reframing is exactly what the apps are built for. The interface is fast. The options are right there. The deposit flow takes seconds. Everything about the environment is optimized for the part of your brain that acts on impulse, not the part that thinks it through. By the time your rational brain has anything to say, you've already placed the next bet.

Two days later, $150,000 was gone.

Two weeks after that, I bet again.

That loop isn't unique to me. It isn't a character flaw or a weakness specific to people who lack discipline. It's what happens when a system designed by behavioral scientists collides with a brain doing exactly what brains are supposed to do, seek reward, avoid loss, fix mistakes. The system wins that matchup almost every time.

There's a clinical framework for this: two systems in the brain, one slow and deliberate, one fast and reactive. Betting apps are engineered to target the fast one. Quick rewards hit before the slow system can intervene. But honestly, the simpler version is just this: when you're in the middle of losing, you stop being the person who understands dopamine loops and start being the person who just needs to fix it. The knowledge doesn't disappear. It just becomes completely irrelevant to what you're actually doing.

I'd studied this. I understood the psychology. I could have explained loss chasing to you in clinical detail while I was actively doing it. None of that mattered.

The other thing that happens faster than most people expect is that betting becomes identity. For a lot of guys I know, placing bets is a social ritual, talking lines with friends, sharing picks in the group chat, having money on the game makes watching it feel like real participation rather than just observation. That sense of belonging is real, and it matters. VIP treatment accelerates it. When someone calls you a "valued customer" and puts you in a suite, you start to feel like you're on the inside of something. Walking away doesn't just mean stopping a habit — it means giving up a role you've started to identify with.

That's the piece most recovery advice misses. You can delete the app, but if you don't replace the underlying need. The adrenaline, the status, the ritual, the escape from whatever else is going on, the void just pulls you back toward something that will fill it. And the app is still on the App Store.

Stress makes all of it worse. Under pressure, the brain defaults to familiar patterns. A stressful week at work or a rough patch in a relationship doesn't just make someone more likely to bet; it makes them more likely to bet badly. Bigger. Faster. Less carefully. Every time my paycheck hit and I saw that number sitting in my account, I felt the pull. It was almost automatic. Money available meant opportunity available, and opportunity available meant the itch.

Not everyone who bets ends up in trouble, and there's no clean way to know in advance which category you're in. Some people bet casually for years and it stays casual. Others hit a trigger point and the escalation happens fast. The research points to a mix of factors — genetics, mental health history, social environment, how early you started, but none of it is deterministic. Someone with every risk factor might be fine. Someone with none of them might spiral quickly.

What does seem consistent is what the way out requires. First you have to see the pattern, really see it, not just know about it abstractly. Then you need structural barriers, not willpower; real friction between the urge and the action. Then you need something to replace the emotional need that betting was filling, because that need doesn't disappear just because you deleted the app.

Willpower alone doesn't work against a product designed by teams of people whose entire job is to keep you betting. I know that from experience. What works is changing the environment so the automatic response is the safer one.

Not glamorous. Just true.

CHAPTER 4

The Perfect Conditions

There's a moment I keep coming back to. A weekday afternoon, nothing dramatic about it. Emails that needed answers. Meeting prep I hadn't done. Instead I found myself opening the app, checking a line that looked interesting, building a small parlay, accepting an offer that had my name on it.

How does that happen? How does a normal Tuesday afternoon become a gambling session?

I placed the bet. Maybe it was $500, maybe $2,000 – the amount changed but the pattern didn't. Sometimes it hit and I felt clever for twenty minutes. Sometimes it lost and I'd think about chasing it later. Either way, an hour had passed and I'd barely noticed. The emails were still there. The meeting prep was still undone. And now part of my attention was locked on a bet running in the background.

That happened more often than I want to admit. The app was always there. The lines were always interesting. The offers always had my name on them.

This chapter is about why. Not why I specifically – why this generation, why a normal Tuesday afternoon in 2024 can turn into a gambling session before you've made a single conscious decision about it. We're living in a particular moment where law, money, technology, and human psychology all lined up in a way that made this kind of behavior feel completely normal. None of it happened by accident.

It started with a court case. In 2018, the Supreme Court ruled in *Murphy v. NCAA* and struck down the federal ban on state-authorized sports betting. Before that decision, legal sports betting was mostly Vegas and a handful of other jurisdictions. After it, states could legalize on their own timeline, and most of them moved fast. Capital flooded in. Apps got built at scale. Companies that had been operating in gray areas suddenly had a legal runway and went after the entire country at once.

The money that followed is staggering. In 2024, U.S. Sports betting revenue hit record numbers as more states came online and the mobile platforms got sharper at keeping people engaged. That revenue funds marketing budgets most industries can't touch, expensive celebrity partnerships, league deals, and the kind of personalized retention strategies I experienced firsthand with Mike.

Then came the league integrations, and this is where it gets subtle.

The NFL, NBA, UFC, all of them started folding betting into the actual viewing experience, not just running ads during breaks. *Integrated.* I remember sitting at a sports bar on a Saturday night, eating wings, watching a UFC card. Normal night out. Between rounds, the live-betting lines were just there on the screen, right next to the fighter stats, the reach numbers, the tale of the tape. Nobody pointed it out. The commentators didn't mention it. It was just part of the broadcast, as natural as the round timer.

That's the shift most people miss. When the league itself frames a bet as part of watching the sport, it stops being a separate activity you choose to do. It becomes part of fandom. Part of being a real fan rather than a casual one. And that normalization has consequences that compound quietly over time.

Social media poured fuel on all of it. The content ecosystem around sports betting is engineered to make gambling look like a wealth strategy. You scroll past a screenshot of a parlay ticket — seven figures, fire emojis, hundreds of comments asking for picks. What that post doesn't show is the hundreds of losing tickets that came before it, or the people who copied the strategy and lost everything trying to replicate one lucky hit.

Then there are the celebrities. Kevin Hart. Jamie Foxx. Athletes. Musicians. Faces you've trusted for years, suddenly telling you this app is where the smart money goes. I'd see those ads and find myself wondering what they're being paid, because whatever it is, it's worth it to the apps. The implicit message is simple: successful people bet. People you admire bet. Why wouldn't you?

And then there's a whole other category. The guys selling picks. Posting their wins, building an audience, charging a subscription for their "guaranteed locks." What they're actually doing is selling pickaxes during a gold rush. They make money whether you win or lose; their business model depends on you believing the edge is real. The more people lose chasing tips, the more desperate the buyers get for the next tout's system.

All of it together, the celebrities, the pick sellers, the integrated broadcasts, the social media screenshots — creates an environment where *not* betting starts to feel like the odd choice. Like you're opting out of something everyone else is already in on.

If you're in your twenties, you're absorbing all of this at the exact wrong time. Your twenties are when you build the financial foundation that either sets you up or sets you back for the next four decades. Savings habits. Investment habits. How you think about money, risk, compounding. A $5,000 loss at twenty-two isn't really a $5,000 loss; it's the compound growth that money would have produced over forty years. It's the down payment that doesn't happen. It's the retirement account that starts five years later than it should have.

I think about the money I lost and I know, not theoretically, but with real certainty; that it would have compounded into millions, not from some lucky investment. Just from time and discipline and leaving it alone. That's what was actually on the table every time I opened the app, not a potential parlay win. The quiet, unglamorous future that money was supposed to build.

The peer pressure piece is real too. When somebody in your circle hits a parlay and brings it up every time you watch a game together, *not* betting starts to feel like opting out of the conversation. The desire to be part of the story, to have something on the game, to have a reason to care beyond just watching — that's social pressure layered on top of everything else. The apps know it. Some of them have literally built social-sharing features into the product, because they understand that the fastest way to acquire a new user is through someone that user already trusts.

Legalization made a few things safer — age verification, anti-money-laundering rules, some consumer protections that didn't exist in the gray-market era. Those matter. But it also removed the friction that used to slow people down. What used to be something you had to actively seek out is now something that seeks you. Regulation got the industry out of the shadows without doing nearly enough to address how the products themselves are designed. Some states are starting to ask about deposit limits and mandatory cooling-off periods. The challenge is that the industry moves faster than anyone trying to regulate it.

The forces didn't meet by chance. Legal permission created investment. Investment created marketing. Marketing created cultural normalization. Normalization combined with psychology and personalized technology created the specific moment we're in, where a normal Tuesday afternoon becomes a gambling session before you've made a single conscious decision about it.

Understanding how that happened doesn't make you immune. But it's where defense starts, because you can't build protection against something you haven't clearly seen. And what the rest of this book is about is building that protection in a way that doesn't depend on out-willing a product designed by people whose entire job is to make sure you don't.

CHAPTER 5

Other People's Money

The thing about losing $150,000 is that it sounds like a lot until you start reading about people who lost a lot more.

I'm not telling you these stories so you can compare yours favorably and feel a little better. I'm telling you because I needed to read them at one point, and they did something for me that nothing else could. They forced me to admit that the protective story I'd been carrying, that I was sharper than this, more disciplined than this, somehow built differently than the people who get destroyed by gambling, was just a story. The math doesn't care about your career. Your IQ doesn't insulate you. Your bank account, however large, is a buffer, not a shield.

Phil Mickelson is one of the best golfers in history. Forty-five PGA Tour wins. Six majors. Hundreds of millions in tournament earnings, hundreds of millions more in endorsements. The kind of net worth that should make somebody gambling-proof in any rational sense.

In 2023 his former associate Billy Walters published a book that put Mickelson's gambling losses at over $100 million across multiple decades. Mickelson didn't deny it. He acknowledged he'd had a problem and was working on it. The numbers in Walters's account included a stretch where Mickelson allegedly placed over a billion dollars in wagers in a five-year window, with bet sizes that started in the tens of thousands and crept into the hundreds of thousands per game. Lines on baseball, basketball, football. Anything moving.

Read that again. Phil Mickelson, with everything he had earned, working with one of the most respected handicappers in history, lost north of nine figures. The kind read is that betting was a hobby and the hobby ate $100 million. The harder read is that even at his level, the same brain math that runs in your phone right now ran in his head, just with more zeros attached.

Pete Rose holds the all-time MLB hits record. He bet on baseball games while managing the Reds. He has been banned from the Hall of Fame for over thirty years because of it. He had to know what he was risking. He bet anyway. The arithmetic of urge versus consequence didn't change because he was a legend.

Charles Barkley once told an interviewer he'd lost more than $10 million gambling, and that the actual number was probably higher. He said it the way you might admit to drinking too much in college, almost casually, not because he wasn't aware of what he'd done but because he'd lived inside it long enough that the weight of the number had stopped registering. He was earning enough that it didn't break him. That isn't a defense. It's a description of a system that doesn't break people who can absorb losses, and absolutely breaks the people who can't.

Tim Donaghy was an NBA referee. In 2007 he pleaded guilty to federal charges related to betting on games he was officiating. Think about that career path. He was a professional whose entire job depended on his integrity, and he risked all of it for what investigators valued at roughly $30,000 in payouts. The math on that decision is so absurd it stops looking like math at all and starts looking like the same instinct that runs in everyone who's ever convinced themselves this one is different.

There are dozens of these. Lottery winners who took home $30 million and lost it all within a decade, often through gambling. Athletes whose careers paid them more in a single contract than most people earn in five lifetimes, broke and borrowing within a few years of retirement. Tech founders who sold companies for hundreds of millions and then spent late nights at private gambling clubs trying to recapture some feeling that the money itself didn't deliver.

The pattern in all of them is the same thing I felt in my own life, just at different scales. The protective belief that whatever happened to those other people couldn't quite happen to you. Until it did.

I find a strange comfort in those stories now, not because I enjoy other people's pain. Because they convinced me that what happened to me wasn't a failure of my specific character. It was a feature of being a human brain interacting with a system designed to exploit the way human brains work. The CEO and the line cook get taken by the same mechanisms. The variables change. The outcome bends in the same direction.

If you're sitting with a loss right now and telling yourself you should have known better, you should have been smarter, you should have been somehow more than what you turned out to be, read those names again. Mickelson. Rose. Barkley. Donaghy. None of them lacked intelligence or resources. None of them woke up wanting to be the cautionary tale. They got there by doing what the system was designed to make them do, one bet at a time, until the math caught up with all of them.

The math is patient. The system is patient. Your turn doesn't have to be next.

CHAPTER 6

What the Industry Won't Tell You

I bought every single one of these.

It wasn't naivety, and it wasn't because I hadn't done the reading. I understood how dopamine worked. I knew the math. I'd watched people around me lose money and told myself I was different. And I still got taken by the same stories the industry sells to everyone who sits down at the table.

So here they are, every myth that kept me in the game longer than I should have been, and what's actually true underneath each one.

Myth 1: If you know sports, you have an edge.

When I was deep in it I genuinely believed my research meant something. I was watching film. I knew injury reports before they went public. I had opinions on coaching tendencies, weather conditions, line movement. I felt like I was doing actual work, like I'd earned the right to bet big because I'd put in the time. It wasn't gambling, it was analysis. That's the story I sold myself.

Then I lost $150,000 in a week picking games I'd studied.

Here's what's actually true. The house edge on a standard bet runs about 4-5%, which means you need to win roughly 52-53% of your bets just to break even — not to profit, just to not lose. And that's before emotional decisions, bad beats, and the times you deviate from your own rules when the pressure gets high enough. The lines are set by people whose entire job is to price games correctly, using data and models that dwarf anything you're working with on your phone. Your football knowledge doesn't move that needle in any meaningful way.

Professional bettors do exist. That part is true. But they operate with massive bankrolls, proprietary models, multiple accounts spread across every book, and teams of analysts grinding tiny edges over thousands of bets. They're also getting limited and banned by the books the moment they start winning consistently. Which tells you everything you need to know about how the industry actually views the concept of a skilled bettor. They'll take your money when you lose and shut you out when you win. That's the whole relationship.

The knowledge myth keeps you at the table because it reframes gambling as a skill game. And once it's a skill game, losing just means you need more practice. More research. One more season of data. The industry never has to sell that story directly; the bettor sells it to himself.

Myth 2: Parlays are the smart play.

I built hundreds of parlays convinced I was being strategic. Small stake, massive potential payout, using my knowledge across multiple games instead of just one. It felt efficient. Like I was maximizing my edge.

We already went through the math: a six-leg parlay at 50% per leg hits roughly 1.5% of the time. One or two wins out of every hundred attempts. The payout sounds enormous until you calculate what you spent getting there. The house keeps a larger cut on parlays than on almost any other bet on the menu, which is exactly why the apps push them constantly. Every parlay-boost notification, every same-game-parlay prompt, every interface feature that makes it easy to add one more leg, all of it exists because parlays are the highest-margin product they sell.

When I was chasing losses, the bets that felt like smart recovery moves were always parlays. Long shots that could erase the damage in one ticket. They always made it worse. The app knew that. It just never told me.

Myth 3: You could go pro if you're disciplined enough.

This one is seductive because it's technically true for a tiny number of people. At my peak I was up $200,000 lifetime. That felt like proof I was on my way. What it actually was, was variance running hot for long enough that I mistook it for skill. The $124,000 parlay I hit in 2024 felt like confirmation. It was luck. My brain recorded it as mastery.

Real professional bettors aren't just disciplined; they're running quantitative operations with infrastructure and capital that casual bettors can't compete with. And even they get limited and banned the moment they become a real threat to the book's margins. The industry tolerates losing bettors indefinitely. It eliminates winning ones. That asymmetry tells you everything.

The "going pro" myth is the industry's most effective long-term retention tool. If you're not profitable yet, it just means you need more experience. More discipline. One more season. So you stay. And while you're staying, the math is doing what it always does.

Myth 4: You're in control.

After I lost $150,000 I understood the psychology of gambling better than most people ever will. I could explain dopamine reward pathways in clinical detail. I knew exactly what loss chasing was and why it was irrational. I had read the papers. I had the vocabulary.

I still bet for another month.

The feeling of control is real. It just isn't accurate. The apps are built by teams whose entire job is to erode your self-regulation at exactly the right moment. Push notifications timed to boredom and stress. Risk-free bets that pay out in site credit instead of real money. Live betting that turns every single play into a new decision before your rational brain can catch up. Intermittent reinforcement — wins that arrive randomly and unpredictably, which neuroscience identifies as the single most addictive reward pattern that exists.

You can know all of that and still open the app. I did it constantly. Control is something you have between sessions, not during them. And the app is designed to make sure there's always another session starting.

Myth 5: VIP treatment means you're winning.

When Mike first texted me, I felt like I'd earned something. Courtside seats. Suite invites. A person whose job was to make sure I was taken care of. It felt like recognition, like the industry was finally acknowledging that I was a different kind of customer.

What I didn't understand yet was what triggered that first text. I'd wagered over $50,000 in a short window and their system flagged me as high-value. Mike's job wasn't to reward me. It was to make sure I kept betting. Every ticket, every suite, every casual friendly text was a calculated investment in increasing my lifetime value to the company.

But here's the part that doesn't get talked about; the part I haven't seen written down anywhere.

After a while I felt an *obligation* to bet, not just a desire. An obligation. Mike had been hooking me up with access, connections, experiences that would have cost thousands if I'd tried to buy them myself. He was generous. He was responsive. He treated me like someone who mattered. And somewhere along the way that generosity started to feel like a debt.

When the urge to stop would come, there was something underneath it that whispered, *but Mike has been good to you.*

Walking away felt like a betrayal of someone who'd shown up for me. The relationship wasn't real in the way I'd come to experience it, but the feeling of owing someone was completely real. And that feeling kept me at the table longer than any odds or any parlay ever could have.

That's the most sophisticated piece of the VIP program, and the part that's hardest to see from inside it. It doesn't just make leaving feel inconvenient. It makes leaving feel *wrong*. Like you're the one breaking something.

If you're getting VIP treatment, it isn't because you're winning. It's because you're losing enough to matter. The perks aren't rewards. They're retention. And the relationship you feel with your host isn't friendship — it's a product designed to feel like one.

Myth 6: It's legal now so it's safer.

Legalization did some real things — age verification, anti-money-laundering rules, consumer protections that didn't exist in the gray-market era. Those matter.

But legal doesn't mean safe. In 2025, Americans wagered over $166 billion on sports. Sportsbooks kept nearly $17 billion of that, a record, up over 20% from the year before. About one in three young adults between 21 and 44 placed their first sports bet before they were legally allowed to. Problem-gambling signs show up in roughly 10% of men aged 18 to 30, double the rate from just a few years ago.

What legalization actually did was remove friction. Something you used to have to go find now comes to you. The industry got legal infrastructure and cultural permission to scale aggressively, and the consumer protections built into that framework were nowhere near enough to address how the products themselves are designed to behave. Legal means taxed and regulated. It doesn't mean the app in your pocket isn't engineered to keep you betting past the point where you should have stopped.

Myth 7: The industry cares about responsible gaming.

Every app has a "Play Responsibly" message somewhere. They offer self-exclusion tools. They run awareness campaigns. They sponsor mental health initiatives. From the outside, it looks like an industry that takes player welfare seriously.

Then they send targeted promotions to accounts showing signs of problematic behavior. Then they make their highest-margin products, parlays, live betting, micro-bets — the most accessible and most aggressively marketed features in the app. Then they build VIP programs specifically designed to deepen the relationship with their heaviest losers.

The self-exclusion tools exist because regulations require them. The responsible-gaming messaging exists because it's good PR and provides legal cover. If player welfare were actually the priority, the product design would look completely different. It doesn't. The business model requires that you keep betting, and everything in the app is built around that single outcome.

Myth 8: At least I'm only hurting myself.

I think about Tom, someone who was once close to me, who lost his house to gambling. The depression that followed scared everyone around him. I spotted him money because I didn't know what else to do. Mutual friends lost sleep over him. None of us were betting. All of us paid a price.

I think about Rose sitting across from me at dinner, trying to talk to me, trying to connect with me, while I was nodding along with money on a game running on my phone under the table. She wasn't gambling. But she was in a relationship with someone who wasn't really there. Distracted, irritable, lying about why. She paid for my problem without ever placing a bet.

I think about my team. Events I organized. Milestones we hit together. Moments that were supposed to matter, while I was standing in a hallway watching scores on my phone.

The "only hurting myself" myth is one of the most useful ones the industry benefits from. It keeps gambling framed as a private matter. It keeps the people around you from feeling like they have standing to say something. It keeps you from feeling like you owe anyone honesty about what's actually happening.

Gambling doesn't stay contained to the person doing it. It bleeds into every relationship, every room you walk into, every conversation where half of you is somewhere else.

I believed all of this. Every single myth, at some point, felt completely true to me.

The one that did the most damage was the last one, the belief that what I was doing was mine alone to carry. That the losses were private. That the people around me weren't affected by something they didn't even know was happening.

They were. They always are.

You don't have to learn that the $150,000 way.

CHAPTER 7

The Stories We Tell

I want to be clear about something before I tell you this story: 2025 wasn't where it started.

By the time I lost $150,000 in a single week, I had four years of history with this. Four years of cycles, resets, wins that felt like proof and losses that felt like temporary setbacks. Four years of telling myself I had it handled. I need you to understand that before we get to San Diego, because the crash didn't happen in a vacuum. It was the inevitable end of something that had been building since I was twenty-two and had no idea what I was actually getting into.

I was twenty-two in 2021 and I was making more money than I knew what to do with. Over $400,000 that year — real money, the kind I hadn't grown up around, the kind that felt almost fictional when I saw the numbers on a screen. I hadn't come from money. Nobody in my family had. So when it started arriving at that level I did what a lot of young guys do when they suddenly have more than they ever expected; I spent it. Traveled constantly. Went out constantly. Lived like the balance in my account was a scoreboard and the point was to run it up.

Spring was my girlfriend at the time. We did long-distance, which meant the time we actually had together was supposed to matter, and it did, to her. What she kept running into was that it mattered less to me than it should have, not because I didn't care about her, but because Sundays had become something else entirely. Multiple games on every screen. My phone in my hand. The constant low hum of attention split between her and whatever game had money on it.

She never said it was gambling, exactly. What she said was that she didn't have my full attention. That when she was there, I wasn't really there. That she could be mid-sentence and watch my eyes go somewhere else.

She was right. I just wasn't ready to hear it.

That year I hit a four-leg parlay for $20,000. I remember the feeling more than I remember the ticket; the pure electric shock of watching the last game cover and realizing what had just happened. Twenty thousand dollars off a single slip. I'd never felt anything quite like it. It didn't feel like luck. It felt like confirmation. Like the universe acknowledging that I'd figured something out most people hadn't.

That feeling is the most dangerous thing in this chapter, not the money. The feeling.

I don't remember exactly how 2021 finished. What I remember is that it ended the way most of those years ended — somewhere in the noise between the wins and the losses, with the wins feeling like skill and the losses feeling like variance and the overall picture staying conveniently blurry.

2022 was the year the pattern became undeniable, or at least it should have been.

I won $40,000 in a single run, not over months. Over a weekend. Games breaking right, every pick landing, the balance climbing in a way that felt less like gambling and more like being paid for expertise. By Sunday night I had forty thousand dollars that hadn't existed on Friday.

By Sunday night I also didn't have it anymore.

The same weekend. The same momentum that built it dissolved it, one bad beat at a time, and I did what the pattern always demanded

— I kept betting to win it back. When the weekend was over I deleted the apps. Told myself I was done. Felt genuine about it.

I always thought about stopping. The thought visited me regularly, seriously, with real weight behind it. And I always tied back in. Because the thing about deleting the apps is that it only addresses the access, not the pull. The pull doesn't live in the app; it lives in you. After a few weeks without it, the pull would find its justification, a big game coming up, a line that looked too good to ignore, a friend mentioning a bet that felt obvious. One download and I was right back where I'd been.

I did that cycle more times than I can count across 2022. Delete. Reload. Win something. Lose more. Delete again.

The relationship with Spring ended in the summer of 2023.

I don't want to reduce four years to a single cause; relationships are more complicated than that. But I know what I was in 2023. I was betting heavily, winning and losing significant money, and I was in a bad headspace, the kind that seeps into everything around you whether you mean it to or not. The kind that makes you present in body and absent everywhere else.

She had been telling me for two years that she didn't have my full attention. In 2023 she stopped asking for it.

After the relationship ended, I kept betting. If anything, the structure that had at least created some friction — the weekends she was there, the arguments that made me aware of what I was doing. Was gone. There was nothing to interrupt the pattern anymore. Just me and the apps and the same cycle running with slightly less resistance.

I was winning and losing large amounts. I was in a bad place mentally. The betting wasn't causing all of it, but it wasn't helping any of it, and I knew that, and I kept going anyway.

That's the thing about this that's hardest to explain to someone who hasn't been in it. You can know something is making your life worse and still not stop. The knowledge and the behavior operate on completely separate tracks. I understood what I was doing. I just couldn't make myself care enough about the future version of me who would have to deal with the consequences.

2024 was the year that sealed my fate for 2025.

That sounds dramatic, but I mean it precisely. If 2024 had been a losing year, I might have stopped. If I'd finished significantly down, I would have had evidence that the cycle wasn't sustainable. Instead, 2024 gave me the worst possible outcome, it confirmed everything I wanted to believe about myself.

I was at my friend's place in Arizona when the parlay hit. Eight legs. I don't remember every game on the ticket, but I remember sitting there watching the last one close out and feeling something shift in my chest. The kind of win that doesn't feel real while it's happening. When the final number settled, I was up $124,000 off a single ticket.

Eight legs. Each one had to hit. The odds of that ticket were astronomical. And it hit.

I finished 2024 up six figures overall. I had a track record that now spanned four years. I had survived the losing cycles and come out ahead. I had evidence — real, documented, numerical evidence, that I was different from the people who lose. That my instincts were sound. That the $200,000 net positive I'd built wasn't variance. It was skill.

I was wrong. But I was wrong with receipts, which is the most dangerous way to be wrong.

Before I tell you what happened next, I want to be clear about something: I wasn't some casual bettor who got in over his head. I'd wagered millions over four years. I had a track record. I had won $124,000 off a single parlay twelve months before the crash. I was up $200,000 net lifetime.

That $200,000 wasn't just money. It was validation. When people talked about professional sports bettors, I could point to my record. I was one of the few who actually came out ahead. The identity; the guy who figured it out, the guy who beat the system — had become as real to me as anything else I'd built.

That's why the week I'm about to describe hit differently than anything that came before it. It wasn't just losing money. It was erasing everything. Going from +$200K to deeply negative in seven days. Destroying the evidence I'd spent four years building that I was different, that I was good at this, that I knew what I was doing.

The money hurt. The identity collapse hurt worse.

It was October 2025. I'd just gotten back from Peru — walked through parts of the Amazon, spent time in the forest, the kind of trip that pulls you completely out of your normal life for a stretch. I came back energized. We'd just brought on two new partners for my sales team and I wanted to mark it properly, build the relationship outside of work. So I flew to San Diego.

Thursday night we were at a steakhouse near the harbor. Nice place. The weather was perfect, the way San Diego weather always is, warm enough to feel like a gift, the harbor visible through the windows, the kind of dinner where everything feels like it's going right. I was having a genuine conversation, present and relaxed, and then between courses I picked up my phone and checked the line for Thursday Night Football.

I put $10,000 on the game.

It hit. Just like that I had $20,000.

One of my partners saw me do it. He looked up from his drink. "You're a fucking wizard."

I showed them the app. The balance climbing. The green numbers. They were impressed. I felt good. It felt easy. It felt like the previous four years of evidence presenting itself right on cue, *see, this is what I do, this is who I am.*

Saturday morning I woke up and immediately opened the app. College football. I threw the entire $20K on one game. It hit. I didn't even wait — I rolled $25K onto an afternoon game. When that one cleared, I had $70,000. Everything felt aligned. The games were lining up exactly how I'd called them. I wasn't guessing. I was flowing. Every bet felt inevitable.

Sunday came. Two more bets. Both hit.

By the end of Sunday I was at $130,000.

That night we were at a bar in the Gaslamp Quarter. I pulled up the app and showed them the balance. $130,000. They were stunned. I felt untouchable, completely at peace, the way you only feel when everything you've built and everything you believe about yourself is being confirmed in real time. I remember thinking *this is what it was supposed to feel like. This is the version of the story that was always coming.*

I thought about cashing out. The thought crossed my mind more than once that weekend. I chose not to.

There's a name for what was happening in my head at that moment. Behavioral economists call it the *house-money effect.* When you're up on a winning streak, your brain quietly reclassifies the winnings as separate from your own money. House money, and you'll risk it on bets you'd never take with your original stake. Richard Thaler, who later won a Nobel Prize for related work, documented this in research published in *Management Science* in 1990. The math between the two situations is identical; the stake just feels different. I had $130,000 sitting in an app and my brain had silently moved most of it into the house-money bucket. The thought of losing it didn't carry the weight that losing my original $10K would have. That mental accounting is exactly what the apps want from you, and it's what eats your bankroll the moment your luck turns.

Thursday came and I was back home. Poker night at a friend's house — guys I hadn't seen in a while who'd randomly reached out, small stakes, $100 buy-in, just a casual game. The kind of night that under any other circumstances would have been exactly what I needed.

I put $20,000 on the Bengals-Steelers game. Steelers to cover the +5.5 spread.

We were playing cards while the game ran on the big screen. I was trying to focus on both, track my hand, track the game; and doing neither well. The Steelers didn't cover.

I got quiet. Nobody noticed why. I threw my poker winnings into the final hand, broke even for the night, said I was tired.

I drove home alone. I didn't sleep. I stayed up until 2am reading stats, looking at matchups, running through every angle I could find — not because I thought it would change anything, but because the only alternative was sitting with what had just happened, and I wasn't ready to do that.

The only thought I had, running underneath everything else: *I have to win it back.*

Friday I flew to Georgia to visit Rose.

Rose and I had been together for a while, and this was the first time I was sitting down to dinner with both her parents, not a casual introduction — a real dinner, the kind where you understand that how the night goes matters. They were warm, genuinely trying to get to know me, asking questions, telling stories. Her dad had this easy way of holding a conversation that made the table feel relaxed. The vibe was good. It should have been one of those nights you remember for the right reasons.

Sports betting wasn't legal in Georgia, so I couldn't use my regular app. I found a workaround, Robinhood had what they called futures trades on sports outcomes. Legally ambiguous. It worked.

I had $20,000 on Miami to beat Louisville before we sat down.

The whole dinner I was nodding, smiling, asking the right questions, doing the surface-level work of being present. But in the back of my head, underneath every exchange, every story, every moment her parents were trying to figure out who their daughter was with, the game was running. I'd check the score under the table when I could. Miami was losing. I kept live-betting. Kept convincing myself they'd come back. By the time her dad was mid-story about something I couldn't focus on, I had $45,000 on that game.

My phone buzzed. I glanced down.

Miami's quarterback had thrown an interception. Louisville won.

I felt it in my chest before I fully processed the number. $45,000. Gone. While her father was telling a story and her mother was laughing and Rose was looking at me the way she does when she's proud of how something is going.

I kept smiling. I kept nodding. I stayed at that table for another twenty minutes and I don't remember a single word anyone said.

After dinner we went back to her parents' house. Old-school setup, separate rooms, which I respected. I went to the guest bathroom and watched the final minutes of the game on my phone alone. The clock running out. The number confirmed. I splashed water on my face and went back out and sat on the couch and watched television with the family like nothing had happened.

Rose could tell I was off. "You okay?" she asked quietly.

"Yeah," I said. "Just a little bummed."

We went to bed. I lay in the guest room staring at the ceiling with $65,000 left from the original $130K and one thought that wouldn't leave me alone no matter how many times I told myself to go to sleep.

I can win it back. I just need to be smarter.

Saturday and Sunday I bet on college football and NFL games. I wasn't following any strategy. I wasn't thinking clearly. I was chasing — pure and simple, the same mechanism I'd described to myself in clinical terms a hundred times, now fully operational and completely beyond my control.

I deposited another $20,000 from my bank account. A few taps. The money appeared instantly. Then it was gone too.

By Monday it was all gone.

I was sitting alone at the Atlanta airport waiting for my afternoon flight back to Vegas. Gate seat. Overhead screens showing scores I no longer had money on. I opened Robinhood.

$0.00.

I deleted it. Then I deleted the betting app. Both of them, gone, right there at the gate.

I put on a Netflix show I don't remember. I didn't sleep on the plane. I just sat there replaying the week. The steakhouse in San Diego, the Gaslamp Quarter bar, the poker night, the dinner with her parents, the bathroom, the ceiling of the guest room, the moment I knew it was over and kept betting anyway.

I didn't tell anyone.

Not Rose, not my partners, not my family. Nobody.

I went back to my life like nothing had happened. Meetings. Work. Normal routines. I was professional and present and completely hollowed out and nobody knew why.

Two weeks later I bet again.

I kept betting for another month. Smaller amounts, same pattern, win a little, lose more, convince myself the next one would fix it. During that month I was checked out at work. I'd look at my phone during meetings. I'd disappear at team events to watch games I had money on. I'd get irritable with Rose when I was losing and she had no idea why, couldn't have known, and that distance I was creating, that emotional static between us, was something I was doing entirely alone.

About a month after the crash I used the app's self-exclusion feature. Banned myself for three months. It was the first structural decision I'd made in years that didn't depend on how I felt in the moment.

The urges didn't disappear. They faded. They're still there now — when my paycheck hits, when I'm watching a game, when I'm around friends who are talking about their bets. The pull is quieter than it was. But it's there.

I haven't bet since the ban.

I've partially recovered the money, not all of it. Some.

What I know now that I didn't know in 2021 when I hit that first four-leg parlay and felt like I'd discovered something, what I know

now that I couldn't have told you in 2023 when the relationship with Spring ended and I kept betting anyway; what I know now that I couldn't even fully absorb sitting at the Atlanta airport staring at $0.00 – is this:

You can't bet your way out of a hole. Every dollar you put in trying to fix it is just a slower way of digging deeper.

The house doesn't care about your track record. It doesn't care about your four-year winning history or your $124,000 parlay or the identity you built around being the guy who figured it out. It just needs you to keep going. And if you keep going long enough, the math does what it always does.

Every single time.

PART TWO

THE SPIRAL

The same week. Over and over.

CHAPTER 8

How Mike's Real Job Worked

Mike was nice. That's the first thing I want to say, because I want you to understand that what made the VIP system work wasn't that Mike was a bad person doing bad things. He probably wasn't. He was probably a guy with a job and a quota and a manager and a bonus structure, and his job and his quota and his bonus structure happened to align in a very specific way against my interests.

The VIP host model didn't appear out of nowhere when sports betting went online. It was lifted, almost wholesale, from the high-roller programs that big land-based casinos have been running for fifty years. In Vegas a host's job is to keep a whale, a customer capable of losing six or seven figures in a weekend, coming back. Comped suites. Front-row seats to whatever's in town. A car to the airport. Personal text messages on birthdays. The whole purpose is to make leaving feel like ending a friendship rather than closing an account.

Online sportsbooks took that model and digitized it. The triggers got faster. Where a Vegas host used to identify whales by walking the floor and reading body language, online VIP teams identify them by software. Wager volume crosses a threshold and a profile gets flagged. Loss patterns suggest someone's about to chase. Within hours, sometimes minutes, a host is reaching out.

In 2022 the New York Times ran an investigation into how DraftKings and other major sportsbooks deploy VIP hosts. Reporters spoke with former hosts and obtained internal materials. The picture they painted was, depending on your angle, either standard sales or carefully designed predation. Hosts were given customer profiles that included loss history, deposit patterns, and behavioral notes. They were trained to reach out at specific times. Paychecks hitting. Big games approaching. Periods of inactivity that suggested a customer might be drifting away. Some hosts described having quotas tied to maintaining or growing their assigned customers' lifetime value. That's the industry term. Lifetime value. Translated into English, it means total expected losses.

A handful of those investigations surfaced specific customer stories. People who had lost six figures, then seven, while their VIP host kept upping the perks. Customers who had attempted to self-exclude, only to receive personal calls from their host pulling them back in with an offer too good to refuse. In one case I read about, a customer who said he'd lost over $300,000 on a single platform described being sent a custom-made jersey by his host the same week he was begging the company to limit his account.

Some states have started looking at this. Massachusetts gaming regulators have asked operators to tighten their monitoring of at-risk customers within VIP programs. New York's regulators have asked similar questions. The industry's response has consistently been some version of: we provide responsible gambling tools, customers can use them whenever they want, our hosts are trained to spot problem behavior. Whether that training actually causes hosts to refer customers to those tools, when their bonus depends on those customers staying active, is a question the data doesn't fully answer.

Here's the part that took me longest to understand. Mike probably did not see himself as harming me. From his angle he was managing a relationship with a customer who voluntarily used his platform. He sent me suite tickets to a game I genuinely enjoyed. He responded quickly when I had a question. He treated me with what felt like respect. None of that was theater on his part. It was his job, performed competently.

The harm wasn't in any single text or any single ticket. It was in the architecture. The architecture used Mike's competence and decency against me, by routing my instinct to reciprocate kindness into continuing to bet on a platform whose business model required me to keep losing.

That's the part I want you to sit with if you've ever been taken care of by a host. The host might be a perfectly fine person. The host's job, in aggregate, across thousands of customers, is to maximize losses. Both of those things can be true. Both of them are.

If you're getting VIP-style attention right now, texts about tickets, custom offers, a person on the platform who knows your name and seems to remember things about you, I'm not going to tell you to be rude to them. Don't be. They're a person. But understand exactly what relationship you're in. You are not friends. You are an asset on their book. The friendliness is real. The structure underneath it is not.

CHAPTER 9

The Same Story

It was around 3am when I started searching.

I was in my house in Vegas, lying in bed, phone above my face in the dark the way you do when you're not really trying to sleep anymore. It had been a few weeks since the crash. I'd deleted the apps. I'd gone back to work. I was doing the surface-level things that make life look normal from the outside while something quieter and harder ran underneath.

I wasn't searching because I wanted information. I was searching because I needed to know if I was the only one. If what had just happened to me was a personal failure specific to some flaw in my character, or if there was a pattern — other people, smarter people, people with more to lose, who had gone through the same thing and come out the other side.

I read until the sun came up.

What I found was worse than I expected, not because the losses were larger than mine, though some of them were, by orders of magnitude. But because the structure was identical every single time. Different incomes. Different backgrounds. Different levels of sophistication and self-awareness. The same sequence running underneath all of it: a win that felt like skill, a loss that triggered the chase, a slow accumulation of damage hidden from everyone who mattered, and a moment of reckoning that arrived too late to stop what had already happened.

The story didn't change. Only the names did.

The first case that stopped me cold was a professional golfer.

According to Billy Walters, a professional gambler who partnered with him for five years, Phil Mickelson lost close to $100 million gambling over three decades, wagering more than $1 billion in total. Mickelson himself confirmed the addiction in a 2022 *Sports Illustrated* interview, calling his gambling reckless and embarrassing and saying he'd spent hundreds of hours in therapy addressing it.

One hundred million dollars.

Sit with that number for a moment, not because it's shocking, but because of what it means for the argument that knowledge and discipline protect you.

This wasn't someone who stumbled into gambling without understanding risk. This was a man who had spent his entire adult life performing under pressure, managing his mental state, making calculated decisions with enormous consequences. Professional golf at the elite level requires a psychological discipline that most people will never develop. You play alone. Every mistake is yours. There's no team to absorb the blame, no coach to call timeout. You develop systems, routines, methods for staying controlled when everything in your body wants to spiral.

And he still lost a hundred million dollars.

What the record showed wasn't a single catastrophic session. It was a sustained pattern over decades, in 2011 alone Mickelson made over three thousand bets, an average of nearly nine per day. Walters alleged he even attempted to place a $400,000 bet on his own team during the 2012 Ryder Cup while competing in it. Not a man who didn't understand the stakes. A man who bet anyway.

There's something specific that happens to high performers when they enter gambling environments. Their skill identity, the belief that competence in one domain transfers to another — becomes a liability. A man who can make a fifteen-foot putt under championship pressure to win millions believes that same nervous system is serving him when he places a $200,000 bet on a game. It feels like the same discipline. It feels like confidence earned through years of work.

It isn't. The golfer's putter responds to technique. The bet responds to math. And the math doesn't care about your major wins.

The detail that stopped me was the bets placed during competition. While performing at the highest level of his sport, money was moving. His attention was split. The same mechanism I recognized from checking scores under restaurant tables. The inability to be fully present in your own life because part of your brain was always somewhere else, was operating in him at a scale I couldn't fathom.

He didn't lose because he was weak. He lost because the system is designed to capture people exactly like him. High confidence. High-stakes comfort. Easy access. And a product that mimics the feeling of elite performance while delivering none of its actual rewards.

I read all of it and felt two things at once: relief that I wasn't alone, and a cold clarity that if someone with that much to lose and that much mental discipline could get taken, nobody was safe.

The next case hit differently because it wasn't about someone at the peak of everything. It was about someone whose luck had come in twice.

Evelyn Adams won the New Jersey lottery not once but twice, in 1985 and again in 1986, taking home a combined $5.4 million. Two wins. Two separate confirmations that luck was on her side. She gambled most of it away in Atlantic City and ended up broke.

The double win wasn't protection. It was the most dangerous possible primer for what followed. Each win reinforced the same cognitive trap: *I have something others don't. The universe is confirming something about me.*

That feeling — of being chosen, of luck running in your direction, is one of the most dangerous states a person can enter a casino in. Because you're not gambling anymore. You're expressing your luck.

When you win, your brain doesn't record it as variance. It records it as signal. *Something happened*, your brain says, and you need to understand what so you can repeat it. That's the learning mechanism doing exactly what it's supposed to do. The problem is that in gambling, unlike almost every other domain, there is nothing to learn from a win. The outcome was random. The brain doesn't accept that. The brain insists you did something right.

For Adams, each lottery win was the worst possible primer for what followed. She hadn't made a smart investment. She hadn't built a business. She hadn't developed a skill. She'd bought a ticket and gotten lucky. Twice. But the $5.4 million felt like validation. It felt like the universe confirming something about her. And that feeling consumed everything that followed.

I understood that feeling from San Diego. When the first parlay legs hit, it didn't feel like chance. It felt like recognition. Like the system was acknowledging that I'd figured something out. Dopamine doesn't distinguish between skill and luck. It just rewards the outcome and tells you to do whatever you did again.

Nobody warned her. Nobody sat down with lottery winners and explained that the feeling of being lucky is a cognitive state that casinos are specifically designed to exploit.

They just hand you the check.

I found the next one somewhere around 1am, scrolling through a recovery forum on my phone in the dark.

He posted under the name "throwaway_broke38." A logistics manager making $110,000 a year. He started with $200 bets on NFL games. Just for fun. Just to make the games more interesting. His words.

Those five words appear in some variation in nearly every story I found that night. They're the on-ramp. They sound so reasonable it's almost impossible to hear them as a warning. Because they're true. A small bet does make a game more interesting. The dopamine spike during a game you have money on is real and measurable. The attention sharpens. The emotional investment increases. What was background noise becomes the most important thing in the room.

That's the product working exactly as designed.

He didn't plan to drain his retirement account. Nobody plans that. What he planned was to have fun, maybe make a little money, and feel the extra engagement that betting provides. What happened instead followed a path so predictable I could diagram it before finishing his post.

First the wins. Early wins are common; some researchers believe platforms are designed to produce them, because a win in the first few sessions rewires the behavior pattern more effectively than any marketing could. He won enough to feel like he understood something. The stakes climbed gradually, the way water heats; you don't notice until it's too late.

Within two years he'd drained $43,000 from his retirement account. Maxed out three credit cards. His mortgage payment bounced.

He told his wife he'd been scammed by a contractor. That's how he explained the missing money. A complete fabrication delivered to the person he shared a life with.

"That's when I knew I had a real problem," he wrote. "I'd become a good liar."

I've read a lot of lines in my research. That one I read twice, lying there in the dark, because I recognized the architecture of it even if the specific details were different from mine. The lying isn't dramatic. It's not a single elaborate cover story. It's a hundred small deflections that accumulate into an alternate version of your financial reality. He didn't wake up one morning and decide to deceive his wife. He made one small omission to avoid a difficult conversation. Then another.

Then another. Until the gap between what she believed and what was true had become so large that the truth felt impossible.

I recognized every step of that, not the specific lies — my situation was different — but the logic underneath them. The way shame builds its own architecture. The way each small concealment makes the next one feel necessary. The way you stop thinking of yourself as someone who is lying and start thinking of yourself as someone who is managing a situation that will eventually resolve itself.

It doesn't resolve itself.

He wrote that even after losing everything, after his wife found out, after the credit cards were maxed, after the mortgage bounced, the urges didn't stop. They just whispered: *one more bet.* As if one bet could undo two years of damage. As if the math would suddenly shift in his favor because he'd suffered enough.

The urges don't negotiate. They don't acknowledge consequences. They just keep presenting the same argument in slightly different forms, waiting for a moment of weakness to find purchase.

I want to tell you about one more case I found that night, because it dismantled the last defense I'd been holding onto.

In 2025, a psychiatrist, the incoming president of the Pennsylvania Psychiatric Society, published a first-person account in *Psychiatric News*, the American Psychiatric Association's own publication. She wrote that despite her wealth of knowledge as a physician she was unable to release herself from the grasp of the apps. Less than a year after downloading her first online casino app she lost her savings, part of her retirement, and almost her home.

She said that admitting she was struggling felt like a betrayal of her own expertise.

A psychiatrist. Someone whose entire career was built on understanding addiction, on helping other people break free from exactly this kind of loop. The clinical knowledge didn't protect her. It just gave her better language for what was happening while it was happening.

She could explain in clinical detail exactly why chasing losses was irrational. She did it anyway. Because the part of her brain generating the urge and the part evaluating the decision were operating on completely separate tracks.

Smart people don't lose less. They just lose with better explanations.

The cases above were ones I found through research. The next one I watched happen in real time.

I'm going to call him Tom. I've changed his name because he didn't ask to be in this book, and because what happened to him is painful enough without his real identity attached to it.

Tom was someone who was once a close friend. We grew apart the way people sometimes do — work pulling in different directions, lives separating gradually until the distance becomes the default. But I knew him well enough to have watched the early stages of what happened to him, and I knew people who stayed close enough to see the rest.

The thing about watching someone spiral from the outside is that you don't see the spiral. You see snapshots. A person who seems fine one month, then seems off the next, then seems fine again. The continuity that makes it a spiral is invisible because you're not living inside their head.

What I saw in Tom's snapshots was a guy who always had a bet running. Always, not in an alarming way at first. Just part of how he engaged with sports, with weekends, with social gatherings. You don't notice it as a problem until you start counting the frequency.

By the time I understood what was happening, Tom had lost his house.

Not lost money on the house. Lost the actual house. The thing he'd worked for and built his adult life around, gone because of betting. I don't know the full number. I'm not sure he even knows the full number, because when you're deep in it the losses blur together, each one absorbed into the next bet that was supposed to fix it.

The thing about a house is what it represents beyond the dollar amount. It isn't a financial instrument. It's the physical proof of a life being built. The address people send mail to. The place you imagine your future unfolding in. When someone loses their house to gambling they don't just lose the asset. They lose the narrative.

What came after was harder to watch than the loss itself. The depression hit him hard. He went dark in a way that scared the people around him. He was having bad thoughts, the kind you don't say out loud easily but that the people close to him could feel in every conversation. I spotted him money to cover bills because I didn't know what else to do. You can't watch someone drown and not throw something.

One study found that about one in five problem gamblers reported suicidal thoughts in the past year. That isn't a side effect — it's a predictable outcome of a system that takes money, takes identity, takes relationships, and then leaves someone alone with the wreckage.

For a while it seemed like Tom had pulled back. He seemed more stable. He was dealing with the fallout but appeared to be getting through it.

Then I was at a friend's house and some mutual people who still kept up with him mentioned his name. The way they said it told me before the words did. It had gotten worse, not back to where it was, worse. The pattern had continued and deepened even after everything that had already happened.

I remember sitting there feeling something I hadn't expected. Not just sadness for him, though that was there. Something closer to recognition. I'd just been through my own version of losing control, my own version of the pull being stronger than the consequences. I hadn't lost a house. But I understood, in a way I couldn't have a year earlier, the specific pain of knowing something is destroying you and being unable to stop anyway. The gap between understanding and stopping. How wide that gap can get.

That's the part that stays with me.

Not the house. Not the depression, not even the bad thoughts, as serious as those were. It's the fact that after all of it; after losing the house, after the darkness, after people showing up to help — the pull was still strong enough to drag him back in.

People hear that and think weakness. Lack of willpower. Some fundamental character flaw. That's wrong. Tom didn't go back because he lacked character. He went back because he never had structural barriers — real external constraints that would stop him from acting on the urge even when every part of him wanted to. The urge doesn't respond to consequences. It responds to friction. Tom didn't have enough friction.

I don't know where Tom is now. I hope he's okay. But I also know that the urge doesn't just go away because the consequences get bad enough. Tom's story makes it impossible to pretend otherwise.

I kept reading after Tom. An Arizona teacher lost $28,000, her daughter's college fund, betting on basketball. An Ohio nurse lost $37,000 and his wife left him. A Florida construction worker lost $52,000, and when his wife found out she took the kids and moved in with her parents. A college student in Georgia drained a $15,000 graduation gift in three months and took out a personal loan to cover it without telling his parents. A woman in Illinois, a financial advisor, someone whose entire profession was built on helping other people protect their money, lost $80,000 over two years betting on sports from her office between client calls.

Every story started the same way: small, fun, manageable. Every story escalated through the same mechanism. Every person hid it from the people closest to them. Every person kept betting to fix it. Every person lost more.

The amounts varied. The professions varied. The gender, the age, the income, the location — all of it varied. The structure didn't.

Here's what I noticed lying there at 3am that the individual stories don't capture on their own: the common thread wasn't the amount lost. It wasn't even the behavior itself. It was the story each person told themselves about why they were different.

Mickelson: my discipline and skill give me an edge. Adams: luck is on my side, twice. The logistics manager: I'm just doing this for fun. The psychiatrist: I understand the psychology so I can manage it. The financial advisor: I know the math so I'll know when to stop. Me: I'm up $200,000 net. I've figured something out.

Every single one of us had a version of the same internal argument. *I am not the person this happens to.* I have something. Skill, luck, knowledge, discipline, awareness, that makes me different from the cautionary tale.

That belief isn't a personality flaw. It's a feature of how human beings process information. We are pattern-recognition machines. We look at our own behavior and construct narratives that explain why we are acting rationally. The more intelligent and self-aware you are, the more sophisticated the narrative becomes. The industry knows this. The industry counts on it. Because as long as you believe you're different, you keep betting. And as long as you keep betting, the math does what it always does.

The house doesn't care who you are. It doesn't care how much you know. It doesn't care how much you've won in the past. It just cares that you keep betting. And if you keep betting long enough, the math catches up. Every single time.

I put the phone down somewhere around 3am with the Vegas dark outside my window and the house quiet around me.

I'd spent hours reading about people who lost everything – millions, houses, marriages, retirement accounts, careers built over decades, and I felt two things sitting there in the silence.

The first was that I wasn't alone, not even close. The second was that none of those people had been alone either. Every single one of them had been certain, at some point, that they were the exception.

That their situation was different. That the next bet would be the one that fixed it.

How many people are out there right now, in the middle of their own collapse, thinking they're the only one? How many people are sitting at dinner, checking scores under the table, convinced no one else understands? How many people are making one more bet right now, certain this time will be different?

Too many. And most of them won't tell anyone until it's too late.

You are not uniquely stupid if you're losing. You are not uniquely disciplined if you're winning. You are a person interacting with a system specifically engineered to keep you engaged until the math catches up. Mickelson, Adams, the logistics manager, the psychiatrist, Tom, and me; we all found that out the expensive way.

You don't have to.

CHAPTER 10

The Cost You Can't Count

The hardest part about losing $150,000 wasn't the money.

I know how that sounds. I know $150,000 is a life-changing amount for most people. It was for me too, in a way. But the actual dollars weren't what broke me.

It was everything else the money represented. It was what I gave up to chase it. It was who I became while I was losing it. It was the version of myself I had to hide from everyone I cared about.

This chapter is about the things that don't show up in the bank account.

Rose and I would be at dinner and she'd be talking about something that mattered to her and I'd be nodding along – present enough to maintain the performance, absent enough that I wasn't really there at all. She'd notice. Of course she noticed. Rose isn't someone you can fool easily.

"Are you okay?"

"Yeah, just work stuff."

That became my default. *Work stuff.* It was the perfect lie because it was just believable enough to end the conversation and just vague enough to cover anything. Distracted? Work stuff. Quiet? Work stuff. Checking my phone for the fourth time in ten minutes? Work stuff.

It wasn't work. It was a game I had $20,000 on. It was a bet running in the background of every moment, pulling my attention away from whatever was actually in front of me.

The worst part wasn't even the lying. It was what I could see her doing in response — trying harder. Asking more questions. Reaching for connection across a distance she couldn't name because I hadn't told her what was causing it. She'd keep talking. She'd keep trying. And I'd keep nodding, split between her and a screen, choosing the screen over and over without ever saying that's what I was doing.

I did that countless times. Dinners. Dates. Conversations that deserved my full attention. All of them half-attended. All of them quietly stolen from her without her knowing why.

There's something that happens when you're losing that I didn't anticipate.

You get mean.

Not dramatically, not in ways that make for a clean story about what happened. Just in the small daily ways that people who love you absorb without understanding. Rose would ask a simple question and I'd respond with an edge that had nothing to do with her. She'd suggest something and I'd shut it down. She'd notice I was off and ask what was wrong and I'd say nothing in a tone that made asking again feel dangerous.

My mood had decoupled from my life. It was connected to whether a bet hit or missed. When I was winning I was fine, generous, present, easy to be around. When I was losing I was someone else. Colder. Shorter. Less patient with everything.

She had no idea why. She just knew that sometimes, for no visible reason, I became a different version of myself. And she kept trying to reach the version she knew, not understanding that version was temporarily unreachable because I had money on a game and couldn't think about anything else until it resolved.

What was happening to her wasn't just hurt feelings. The research on partners of problem gamblers documents real, measurable effects: elevated rates of depression, anxiety, chronic stress, and what some clinicians call *concealment fatigue*, the cognitive load of sensing a partner is hiding something without being able to name what it is. A 2019 review in the *Journal of Gambling Studies* summarized findings showing that partners of disordered gamblers report clinically significant depressive symptoms at roughly two to three times the population rate, and that the symptoms persist even after the gambling stops. I didn't know any of that at the time. If I had, I might have understood that the cost I thought was contained inside my account was already being paid by someone else, in a currency she wasn't telling me about either.

I hated who I was in those moments. I just couldn't stop being him, because stopping would have required telling her what was actually happening.

I run a company. Part of what that means is showing up — for the team, for the culture, for the moments that make people feel like what they're doing matters. Team events. Milestones. Celebrations. I organized those things because I believed in them.

I can't tell you how many of them I spent hiding in a hallway.

I'd put the event together, show up, make sure it started right, and then disappear to some corner where nobody would notice I was gone, not because I didn't care. Because I had money on a game and I couldn't be fully present until I knew the outcome. I'd check the score. Get anxious. Check again. Miss entire conversations. Miss moments I'd organized specifically because I knew they mattered.

People would find me and ask where I'd gone. *Work call*, I'd say. Always work call.

I was standing in a hallway staring at my phone watching a game I didn't even genuinely care about, for a bet I'd placed because the line looked interesting on a Tuesday, and I was missing something real to do it.

Sophie Leroy, an organizational psychologist now at the University of Washington, has a name for what was happening to me in those moments. She calls it *attentional residue*. The cognitive cost of switching between tasks. Her research, originally published in *Organizational Behavior and Human Decision Processes* in 2009, shows that when you partially leave one task to start another, a piece of your attention stays stuck on the first one, and your performance on the second task degrades measurably until the first is fully resolved. I wasn't half-attending to my team events because I didn't care; I was attending at maybe 60 percent because the other 40 percent of my brain was permanently allocated to a game running in the background. Multiply that across hundreds of meetings and milestones over four years and the cost stops being abstract. It's not just that I was distracted. I was actively worse at my job, by a margin my team felt without ever knowing what was causing it.

My mom doesn't know any of this.

She immigrated here from one of the poorest countries in Europe at the time, with my brother, with almost nothing. My dad left. So she worked two jobs, sometimes more, making $10, maybe $15 an hour, for years. Building a life out of what most people would look at and say wasn't enough to build anything. She never complained about it in a way that made us feel like a burden. She just worked. She just showed up. Every single day, she showed up.

I grew up watching that. Watching someone give everything they had for people she loved without asking for anything back.

If she knew I'd lost $150,000 in a week, that I'd wagered millions over the years, that I'd sat at a dinner table with Rose's parents with $45,000 on a game running under the table, it would devastate her, not because she'd be angry. Because she wouldn't be able to make sense of it. She'd look back at everything she sacrificed and wonder where it went wrong. She'd feel it as her failure somehow, this thing that has nothing to do with her and everything to do with systems designed to capture people exactly like me.

So I haven't told her. I probably never will.

The money she made in a month, I lost in a single bet without blinking. I've thought about that more than I've let myself admit.

Rose still doesn't know the full number.

I told her about the $45,000 – the Miami game, the dinner with her parents, what I was doing under that table while her dad was trying to get to know me. That conversation was hard enough. I told her I was stopping because it was consuming too much of my time and energy, which was true as far as it went.

I didn't tell her about the other hundred thousand. I didn't tell her I'd been up $200,000 before it evaporated. I didn't tell her I kept betting for another month after I promised myself I'd stopped.

She knows I had a problem. She doesn't know how deep it went.

Here's what I've learned about hiding something like this: you don't have to construct elaborate lies. You just don't mention it. You deflect. You redirect. You let people assume things are fine because you're not saying otherwise. It isn't active deception; it's more like living in a lower-energy state. You're not putting effort into lying. You're just not putting effort into telling the truth.

But it compounds. Every conversation where you stay quiet. Every dinner where you perform fine. Every time someone asks how you are and you say good, knowing that's not the honest answer.

The gap between who you actually are and who people think you are gets wider over time. And at some point you stop being sure which version is real.

Even when I wasn't betting I was thinking about betting.

In meetings, part of my brain was running through possible bets for the weekend. At the gym, I was thinking about a game that night. Lying next to Rose in bed, instead of being present with her, I was replaying a loss or building the next ticket in my head.

The addiction doesn't just take your money. It takes your attention. Your presence. Your ability to be fully inside the moments that actually matter. And the people around you feel that absence even when they can't name what's causing it. They just know something is missing. They just know you're not quite there.

There's a disconnect that happens when you're deep in this that I still find difficult to explain.

I'd hesitate over spending $50 on something in a store. Think about whether I actually needed it. Put it back on the shelf. Then go home and place a $20,000 bet without a second thought.

The money attached to a bet didn't feel real while it was in play. It was just numbers on a screen, just a potential outcome, just an abstraction. Only afterward, when it was gone, did it become real again. Did it become the thing it actually was: money that existed, money that had been earned, money that was now gone.

That disconnect is what removes the natural brake. $20,000 on a game is just a number. $20,000 for anything tangible feels enormous. The math is identical. The emotional weight is completely different. And the industry knows that. The industry built an experience specifically designed to keep the money feeling abstract for as long as possible.

When people ask what gambling cost me they expect me to say $150,000.

That's the easy number. The one that fits in a sentence.

The real cost was the months I spent emotionally unavailable to people who deserved better. It was the version of myself I became when I was losing, irritable, dishonest, somewhere else even when I was standing right there. It was the trust I quietly eroded with Rose by hiding something that significant. It was my mom; two jobs, $15 an hour — who will never know because knowing would hurt her in a way that has nothing to do with what she did and everything to do with how much she gave.

The $150,000 is quantifiable. The rest of it is harder to measure but it doesn't stop being real just because there's no number attached to it.

The urges didn't stop when I stopped betting.

They faded. They got quieter. But months later they're still there — when my paycheck hits and I see that number in my account, when I'm watching a game and the people around me are talking about their bets, when I'm tired and my phone is in my hand and an ad appears at exactly the right moment of weakness.

I have to make the choice, over and over, not to act on it.

I'm not telling you this to make you feel sorry for me. I made my choices. I knew what I was doing even when I couldn't stop doing it.

I'm telling you because the cost isn't just what you see in the account. It's in every dinner you weren't really at. Every conversation you were half inside. Every person who tried to reach you while part of you was somewhere else entirely.

The people around you can feel that absence even when they don't know what's causing it. Even when you're sitting right across from them, they can feel the distance.

And the longer you carry it alone, the heavier it gets.

CHAPTER 11

What I Cost

I want to take a chapter to talk about the people I haven't talked enough about. Not because their stories are mine to tell, but because the real cost of what I did wasn't sitting in any account balance. It was sitting in rooms I walked through without seeing.

Tom

Tom isn't his real name. The story is.

I met Tom in my early twenties. He was a few years older. He'd built something successful, sold it, and at the point I came into his life he was doing what a lot of guys do after their first big exit. Figuring out what to do next while spending more money than was probably wise. He bet because he'd always bet. He bet bigger than most people because he could. For a while he won. He was the guy in our group everyone went to for picks, and he played the part well. Easy with money, generous with information, the kind of person whose attention felt like an endorsement.

Then it ended in a way I'm still not sure I've fully processed.

He needed cash. I don't know exactly why. The math behind it was something he never fully explained to me and probably never fully explained to himself. But he needed it fast. He took out a loan against his house. A real loan, with a real lien on a real property he had bought with money he had earned. The kind of paperwork most people sign once in their lives, if at all, and treat with the gravity it deserves.

The money he borrowed didn't go into a business. It went into bets. He didn't stretch it across months and chip it away gradually. He put it down. Most of it. The way a guy puts something down when he's already convinced himself the next call is the one that turns it.

It didn't turn. It went the other way, and there was no second move available to make.

When the loan came due he couldn't pay it. The bank doesn't care about the story. The bank cares about the lien. He lost the house.

That sentence took me a long time to understand. It still doesn't sit right when I write it. He had built something. He had sold it. He had bought a house with the proceeds. And in a window so short I can't even point at it cleanly on a calendar, he turned the house into a number on a screen, and the number went to zero, and he was somewhere with his stuff in a car trying to figure out what came next.

When the depression came after, it scared people. Tom was not the kind of person who got depressed, in the same way you might say someone is not the kind of person who gets sick. He was always the most stable one in any room. To watch him become someone who didn't pick up the phone, who would disappear for two weeks and reappear with no explanation, who looked physically smaller in a way I can't fully describe, was something I wasn't prepared for.

I gave him money. Several times. I'm not proud of how I did it. I treated it like a transaction, sent it without enough conversation, told myself I was helping. What I was actually doing was protecting myself from having to sit with how scared I was for him. The money was easier than the conversation.

I don't know exactly where he is now. I have a guess. I don't think I've earned the right to write more about him than this.

Rose

I've already told the story of the dinner with her parents and the bet running on my phone under the table. I want to say more about her, because that one scene doesn't capture what she actually carried during the worst of it.

Rose is in medical school. People say med school is hard the way they say the ocean is deep. Accurate but not really informational. The actual texture of it is study hours that would be illegal to ask of any other employee in any other industry, debt accumulating in numbers that look almost theoretical, a future that doesn't really begin until your late twenties or early thirties. She was carrying all of that while I was sitting across from her placing bets between bites of food.

Here's what I never said to her at the time, because saying it would have required acknowledging it.

The $45,000 I lost during a single dinner with her parents was almost exactly what she paid for one year of medical school. Her tuition. Her books. The stipend gap. The year of life she traded to be there. I lost that on a Sunday afternoon in a single sitting, while pretending to listen to her dad ask about my career.

I never said the math out loud to her. I should have, not for guilt, not for performance, but because she deserved to hear me name what I had actually done in terms she would feel. I think she suspected. I'm not sure she'll ever know exactly. I'm not sure I'll ever fully tell her.

My Mom

This is the one I think about more than I should.

My mom worked two jobs for years. The kind of work that doesn't show up on a resume in any glamorous way. Service work. Hours that started before sunrise. The kind of bone-deep tired that becomes invisible because there's no other option. She did it so I could go to a school she couldn't have afforded otherwise. She did it so when I came home for the summer there would be food in the fridge that I didn't have to think about. She did it so the version of me that grew up to lose $150,000 in a week could exist in the first place.

She doesn't know about the money. She doesn't know about the losses, or San Diego, or the airport, or any of it. The version of me she knows is the version of me she helped build, which is the version that turned out fine. The other version, the one that wrote this book, is one she'll probably never meet. I'd rather she not meet him.

I carry that, not as something I'm trying to resolve. Just as a private weight. Some debts you don't pay back to the person who's owed them. You pay them by not making the same choice the next time.

The Team

I've referred a few times in this book to my team. I want to give that some more shape.

I built a company. People worked there. They worked hard, in a lot of cases harder than I did, while I was doing the work but also doing the bets. I missed parts of milestones we hit because I was somewhere else. I was short with people for reasons that had nothing to do with anything they did, because a game had gone the wrong way and I was carrying that into a meeting where they were trying to do their jobs. I ducked into hallways at company events to check scores I couldn't even tell you now. I gave less of myself to people who deserved more.

I didn't lose a single one of them, that I know of, because of the gambling. I want to give myself partial credit there. But I gave them a worse version of their boss than they should have had. That's also a cost. It just doesn't show up on a balance sheet.

What $150,000 Could Have Been

I want to do one piece of arithmetic before I close this chapter, because the dollar amount on its own is almost too abstract to feel.

If I had taken that $150,000 at twenty-six and put it into an index fund tracking the S&P 500, leaving it untouched, the historical average return suggests it would have grown to roughly $2.3 million by the time I was sixty-five, assuming an 8 percent annualized return. That's the conservative version. If I'd added even modest monthly contributions on top of it, the number gets meaningfully larger.

The $150,000 wasn't the loss. The loss was $2.3 million. It was a down payment on a future I quietly chose not to build, in exchange for a feeling that lasted, what, a few weeks at most before it became something I had to forget.

That's what I think about now when the urge cycles through, not the immediate $50 or $500 the bet would cost. The compounding shadow of what that money never gets to become.

It's a quieter calculation. It also actually works.

CHAPTER 12

The Hotline Paradox

You know what I never did after losing $150,000? Call 1-800-GAMBLER.

The thought never crossed my mind, not when I was sitting at the Atlanta airport staring at a $0 balance. Not during the month of continued betting when I knew I had a problem but couldn't stop, not when I finally hit the wall hard enough that something had to change.

I just never called.

You want to know why? Because I had no idea what would happen if I did. What comes after the call? Do they send someone to your house? Do they make you go to meetings? Do they tell your family? I didn't know, and I didn't want to find out.

But the deeper truth is that calling a hotline means admitting you have a problem. And I wasn't ready to admit that. I still thought I could handle it on my own. I thought I was smarter than this. I thought I just needed to be more disciplined, more careful, more strategic next time.

That belief, that I could fix it myself, kept me trapped longer than anything else.

There was another reason I didn't call, one that's harder to explain. I wasn't some casual bettor who got in over his head. I'd wagered millions. I'd been up $200,000 net. I'd had a VIP host texting me courtside seats. I'd convinced myself for four years that I was different — not a gambler in the problematic sense, but someone who understood the game well enough to come out ahead.

How do you call a gambling hotline and explain that? That you were winning for years, that you were genuinely good at it, that you had a track record and a system and real evidence, and then lost control and wiped out everything in a week? That doesn't fit the script of "I need help." It sounds more like "I'm successful at this but had one bad week." Which is exactly what part of me was still telling myself.

So I didn't call. I told myself I'd stop on my own. I made promises. I deleted the apps. I re-downloaded them two days later.

That's the cycle. And a phone number at the bottom of a betting app doesn't interrupt it.

What I did instead was go online. The night after I got back from Atlanta I started searching. "how to stop gambling," "why can't I stop betting," "dopamine and gambling addiction." I read until I couldn't keep my eyes open. Then I did it again the next night. And the night after that. I found forums where people shared their stories anonymously, clinical papers on behavioral addiction, articles explaining exactly how the apps were engineered to keep me in the loop. I got obsessed with understanding what was happening in my brain.

The information helped. Understanding the dopamine mechanism, recognizing the loss-chasing pattern laid out in clinical terms, seeing my own behavior reflected back through other people's stories, it gave me a vocabulary for what I was experiencing. It made me feel less like a uniquely broken person and more like someone caught in a well-documented system.

But it didn't stop me from betting.

Knowledge doesn't equal control. I knew all the right things. I could explain to you in detail why chasing losses was irrational. I understood the psychology. I had the vocabulary. I still opened the app. I still placed the bets. I still told myself this time would be different while doing the exact same thing I'd done a hundred times before.

That's the gap traditional resources don't address. They give you information. They explain the risks. They tell you gambling is dangerous. But they don't tell you what to do at 9pm on a Thursday when your paycheck just hit and every cell in your body is telling you that this time will be different and the app is right there and the line looks right and you've been good for two weeks and one bet won't hurt.

Information doesn't live in that moment. The urge does.

The real reason I didn't tell anyone — not a hotline, not Rose, not my partners, not my family, was embarrassment. I'd built a successful company. I made real money. I was supposed to have my life together in a way that made sense to the people around me. How do you tell people you lost $150,000 in a month betting on games? How do you explain sitting at a dinner table with Rose's parents, trying to make a good impression, while secretly losing $45,000 on your phone under the table?

You don't. You hide it. You tell yourself it's temporary. You convince yourself you can fix it before anyone finds out. And the shame of that hiding becomes its own trap, because the longer you carry it alone, the more impossible it feels to put down.

Shame is what keeps people trapped at exactly the moment they most need to reach out. It's what turns a problem into a secret. It's what makes a hotline feel impossible to call even when you're drowning, because calling means saying the words out loud, and once you say them they become real, and once they're real you have to deal with what that means.

So you don't call. You handle it alone. Until you can't anymore.

The other thing that bothers me about how these resources are structured is that they were built for a different era. Designed for people going to physical casinos, meeting bookies in person, whose gambling required effort and physical presence and a deliberate choice to show up somewhere.

They weren't built for someone lying on their couch at midnight with a betting app on their phone, placing $25,000 on a game they don't even care about just because they need to feel something other than what they're feeling.

The old model of recovery assumes geography. Stay away from casinos. Don't go to the track. Remove yourself from the physical environment where gambling happens.

But what do you do when the environment is your phone? When every sports broadcast has live odds running alongside the score? When your feed is full of parlay screenshots and fire emojis? When your friends are talking lines every Sunday and not betting feels like opting out of something?

You can't avoid the casino when the casino is in your pocket every hour of every day.

There's also an age problem the traditional model doesn't account for. A twenty-two-year-old who just lost $50,000 betting on his phone is not going to respond to the same recovery framework as a fifty-five-year-old who's been going to casinos for decades. Young people don't just need to be told gambling is bad. They need to understand specifically how the apps are designed to manipulate them; the notification timed to boredom, the risk-free bet that gives site credit instead of real money, the VIP host who texts you like a friend but works for the company taking your money.

They need help that speaks to their actual reality, not generic messaging about willpower and moral failure, not a pamphlet. Real, specific, practical strategies for dealing with a product engineered by behavioral scientists to keep you engaged indefinitely. And they need to hear it from people who've been through it — not counselors reading from a manual, but people who lost the money, felt the shame, hid it from everyone they cared about, and found a way out anyway.

The system we have treats gambling addiction like it's entirely the gambler's responsibility to recognize the problem and seek help. But that's backwards. By the time someone is ready to admit they have a problem, the damage is usually already catastrophic. What needs to change is earlier intervention — deposit limits that actually mean something, cooling-off periods built into the product, algorithms that flag problematic behavior and force a pause instead of sending a promotional offer. We need parents to understand that their kids have a casino in their pocket. We need employers and schools to talk about this the way they talk about other behavioral health issues. We need friends to feel like they have standing to say something when they see the pattern.

And we need people who've been through it to tell the truth about what it actually looks like, not the cleaned-up version. Not the redemption arc with a tidy ending. The messy, ongoing, uncertain reality of trying to stay away from something your brain keeps finding reasons to go back to.

I didn't have a solution yet. I couldn't fix the system or the industry or the product designed to keep me coming back. What I could do was stop pretending the problem wasn't mine to deal with.

I was finally tired of not trying.

PART THREE

THE EXIT

Not a cure. Just a door.

CHAPTER 13

The Moment It Became Real

Recognition doesn't arrive with trumpets. It doesn't announce itself. It doesn't wait for you to be ready.

For me it came from someone who had no idea they were delivering it.

I was in Cabo with a group of coworkers and friends, a few days away, the kind of trip that happens when business is going well and everyone needs to decompress. Good energy, good weather, the kind of easy time together that reminds you why you built what you built. We'd had dinner and ended up at a fire pit on the beach, a group of us sitting around the kind of fire that makes conversation feel more honest than it usually does.

Matt was talking.

Matt is someone I've looked up to for a long time, respected in my business, the kind of person whose opinion lands differently than most because he's earned the right to have one. He was talking about people he knew. Stories he'd watched play out from the outside. Men who had gone broke chasing money they didn't need, losing money they already had. He'd seen it happen more than once, he said. Different people, different amounts, same pattern every time. They always thought they were close to turning it around. They never were.

He wasn't talking about me. He didn't know anything about the $150,000. He didn't know about San Diego or Georgia or the Atlanta airport or the month of betting that followed. He was just telling stories by a fire on a beach in Cabo, the way people do when the conversation gets honest.

I sat there and acted like I always do when something hits me harder than I want to show. Relaxed. Nodding. Present enough to seem like I was just listening to an interesting story about someone else.

But his words were already inside me, rearranging things.

Chasing money they didn't need. Losing money they already had.

I'd heard versions of that idea before. I'd read it in the clinical papers I'd been doom-scrolling through at 3am in Vegas. I'd understood it intellectually the way you understand something that applies to other people. But sitting by that fire, with the ocean behind us and Matt's voice carrying the weight of people he'd actually watched fall apart, it landed differently. It landed like a fact about me specifically. Like he was reading something off a page I'd written myself.

I didn't say anything. I didn't confess. I didn't pull him aside afterward and tell him he'd just described the last four years of my life with more accuracy than I'd managed in all the hours I'd spent trying to understand it myself.

I just sat with it. Let it settle. Felt it become something I couldn't unfeel.

The thing about patterns is that you don't see them from inside them. You experience each moment as isolated, each bet a separate decision, each loss a piece of bad luck, each promise to stop a genuine commitment that somehow never holds. The pattern only becomes visible when something forces you outside your own perspective long enough to look back at it.

Matt did that without knowing he was doing it.

On the flight home I thought about what he'd said more than I thought about anything else, not analyzing it. Just letting it sit there in the quiet of the cabin, taking up space, refusing to shrink back into something manageable. I thought about the $130,000 I'd had in an account and watched disappear. I thought about Rose at that dinner table, her parents trying to get to know me while I was somewhere else entirely. I thought about the month of smaller bets after the crash, the promises I'd made and broken so many times they'd stopped feeling like promises.

Chasing money I didn't need. Losing money I already had.

That was the whole story in one sentence. Everything I'd been doing for four years, every story I'd told myself about why it made sense, every identity I'd built around being the guy who came out ahead — all of it collapsed into eleven words said by someone who didn't even know my name was in them.

Here's what I've come to understand about recognition: it doesn't require a dramatic moment. It doesn't require hitting a bottom so low that you have no choice but to look up. Sometimes it just requires someone saying a true thing out loud in a context where you can't immediately argue with it, and your own silence doing the rest.

I'd known for a while. I think some part of me had known for longer than I wanted to admit. But knowing and seeing are completely different things. You can know something and keep it at arm's length, keep it theoretical, keep it about other people and other situations. Seeing it means it's yours. It means you're the person in the story.

There's a clinical literature for the gap I'm describing. Researchers call it the *knowing-doing gap*, or in older philosophical terms, *akrasia*. The well-documented finding that knowing something intellectually and acting on it operate on different cognitive tracks. Stanford's Jeffrey Pfeffer and Robert Sutton wrote a book on the corporate version of the problem in 2000. In addiction research specifically, the gap is sharper still: studies of people in early recovery consistently show that intellectual recognition of the problem typically precedes behavioral change by months, sometimes years. Recognition is necessary but not sufficient. What seems to bridge the gap, according to the research, is some form of external accountability or environmental change that makes acting on the new knowledge structurally easier than continuing the old behavior. Matt didn't fix anything that night in Cabo. He started a clock that I still had to run out on my own.

Sitting by that fire in Cabo I finally saw it.

Not because Matt told me something I didn't know. Because he told me something I'd been refusing to see, in a moment where I had nowhere to put it except directly in front of me.

The signs were never subtle once I let myself look at them honestly. Waking up and reaching for my phone before I was fully awake, not for messages, not for news, but for scores. For results. For confirmation of whether I was up or down before the day had even started. Mood tied to outcomes I'd bet on rather than anything actually happening in my life. People around me feeling a distance they couldn't name because I was always partially somewhere else, mentally running calculations while physically present in rooms that deserved my full attention.

The money disconnect that should have alarmed me earlier than it did, hesitating over $50 in a store while placing $20,000 on a game without a second thought. The number on a bet didn't feel real until it was gone. Then it felt like exactly what it was.

And the cycle that repeated so many times I'd stopped counting. Lose. Promise to stop. Feel briefly better for having made the promise. Wait. Find a reason the next bet was different. Bet. Lose. Repeat. Each time I genuinely believed I'd learned something. Each time I found myself back in the same place with a slightly shorter fuse and a slightly larger hole.

If you're reading this and something in it is recognizable — not as a story about someone else but as a description of something you're currently living, here's what I want you to understand.

You don't have to wait for a fire pit in Cabo. You don't have to wait for someone to accidentally describe your situation out loud before you're allowed to acknowledge it. The pattern is already visible if you're willing to look at it directly. The question is whether you're ready to stop giving yourself reasons why your version is different.

Your version probably isn't actually different. I know how that sounds. I'm not trying to be harsh. It's just the single most useful sentence I can put in front of you, because the belief that you're the exception is what kept me at the table for years longer than I should have stayed.

I recognized the problem clearly for the first time on that trip. I came home and I still didn't stop immediately. Recognition doesn't work like a switch. It works like a slow light coming on; first you can just barely see the edges of things, then gradually the whole room becomes visible and you can't pretend you don't see what's in it.

But it was the beginning of the end of the lying. And that turned out to be the thing that mattered most.

The next step wasn't a feeling. It was a decision. And decisions, unlike feelings, don't depend on how you feel when you make them.

CHAPTER 14

Structure Over Willpower

Recognition wasn't enough to stop me.

I knew I had a problem. I'd lost $150,000 in a week. I understood the psychology of loss chasing. I'd sat by a fire pit in Cabo and heard someone accidentally describe my life in one sentence and felt it rearrange something inside me. I came home with clarity I hadn't had before.

And I still bet for another month.

That's the gap nobody tells you about. Between seeing the problem and stopping the behavior there's a stretch of time where you know exactly what you're doing and do it anyway. The clarity doesn't make you stop. It just makes you feel worse about not stopping. Which, if you're not careful, becomes another reason to bet.

Every morning after the crash I'd wake up with conviction. *Today I'm done. I've learned my lesson.* That conviction would hold until stress arrived. Or boredom. Or a game would start and something in me would say just a small one, just to have something on it, I'll be smarter this time. And I'd believe it. Every single time I'd believe it.

Motivation is a feeling. Feelings change. Willpower is a resource that depletes, and the apps are specifically designed to wait you out — to find you at the moment your resistance is lowest and meet you there with exactly the right offer. Trying to out-will a product built by behavioral scientists is like trying to win an argument with someone who wrote the script. You're not going to win on feeling. You need structure. Things that don't depend on how you feel at 9pm on a Thursday when your paycheck just hit and the line looks right.

That understanding changed everything, not immediately. But it pointed me toward the only approach that actually worked.

About a month after the crash I told Rose.

Not the full truth. I didn't sit her down and walk her through four years of cycles and the $150,000 and the month of continued betting afterward. I brought it up the way I bring up most things I'm not fully ready to confront — casually, almost like a joke, brushing it over before it could become a real conversation. I told her about the $45,000 I'd lost during dinner with her parents. Kept it light. Made it sound like a bad beat, an anomaly, something already behind me.

She didn't react the way I expected.

Rose is in medical school. She works as hard as anyone I know and carries the kind of debt that keeps you up at night, the kind that stretches years into the future before it starts to ease. She didn't say any of that out loud in that moment. She didn't need to. I could feel it land on her, the quiet calculation of what that number meant in her world. What $45,000 could have done for her tuition. What it represented in terms of years of work and sacrifice and deferred everything.

I'd said it like it was nothing. To her it wasn't nothing. And I could see that in her face even as she tried to keep her reaction measured.

She was worried. Not angry, worried. The way you get worried about someone you love when you realize something they've been minimizing might be more serious than they're letting on.

I told her I was stopping. That it was consuming too much of my time and energy. Those words were true as far as they went. They just didn't go very far.

Saying it out loud to her, even the partial version, even dressed up as casual, made it real in a way the internal promises never had. I'd made those promises to myself a hundred times and broken every one. Saying it to Rose, watching it register on her face, feeling the weight of what I wasn't saying sit in the room between us, that was different. That was accountability I couldn't quietly walk back.

I told a few close friends around the same time. No details. Just that I was done, that it had been taking over, that I needed to step away. Most of them were supportive. A couple didn't fully get it. That was fine. The point wasn't their reaction. The point was that I'd said it out loud to people who knew me, which made going back feel like something more than just breaking a private promise.

Then I built the actual barriers.

The first thing I did was go into the app and ban myself. Three months. Self-exclusion, not because I thought three months would fix anything — I knew it wouldn't. But it was the longest option available and I needed distance more than I needed anything else. I needed to remove the option entirely so that in the moments when every part of me wanted to place one more bet, the door was simply closed.

The moment I clicked that button something shifted. It wasn't dramatic. There was no flood of relief. But something that had been available to me every hour of every day was suddenly unavailable, and that absence had weight.

During those three months there were plenty of moments where I thought about workarounds. Another platform. A friend's account. Anything. What stopped me every time was friction. I'd have to actively circumvent the ban. Search for something new, create an account, re-enter payment information, go through verification. By the time I'd mentally walked through all of that, the urge had usually peaked and faded. Barriers don't remove urges. They create space between the urge and the action. In that space, if the barrier is real enough, you can make a different choice.

I deleted every app, not just the one I'd banned myself from, all of them. Every betting platform, every casino game, every poker app, everything that turned money into dopamine with a few screen taps. Looking at my phone and seeing those empty spaces felt strange at first. Like something was missing. After a few days it started to feel like reclaiming something instead.

I almost re-downloaded them multiple times in the first few weeks. The friction stopped me each time — searching, re-entering information, going through verification. By the time I'd gone through all of that, the urge had usually lost its edge, not a perfect system. Enough of one.

I went through every browser and every device and deleted every saved payment method. This one sounds small and it isn't. Betting platforms rely on saved cards because when payment is automatic the decision feels weightless; it doesn't register as a real choice. Removing that automation made every transaction conscious again. Manually entering a 16-digit card number, expiration date, CVV, and billing address is friction. It's a forced pause. It's ten seconds where your rational brain can catch up to what your impulse brain is trying to do. I also unlinked my bank accounts from any payment service that made instant transfers easy.

When urges hit, especially on paycheck days when I could see money sitting in my account and the old voice would start; I'd stop and sit with it. I'd found some meditation guidance online and it gave me a framework for something I'd started doing instinctively. Instead of fighting the urge or distracting myself or white-knuckling through it, I'd just notice it. Let it be there without acting on it. Sometimes I'd drop and do push-ups. Sometimes I'd go for a walk. Anything physical that gave the nervous energy somewhere to go besides an app.

The urge to bet is just a feeling. It's not a command. It rises and if you don't feed it, it passes. Sometimes in five minutes. Sometimes it takes longer. But it always passes. That was the most important thing I learned in those three months — not that the urges would go away permanently, but that they had an end. They weren't permanent states. They were waves. And you could wait them out.

I couldn't just remove betting and leave empty space. The brain fills voids, and if you don't choose what fills them you default back to what you know. So I replaced deliberately. The gym — heavy lifting, running, pushing myself physically. The endorphin hit was real and gave me something to chase that wasn't variance. Pickup basketball with friends. Ping pong. Golf. Anything competitive that didn't have a house edge. And the business, I channeled the energy that used to go into betting into scaling, closing deals, building new revenue. Each business win felt better than any bet because it compounded instead of evaporating. Because it was real.

The barriers weren't impenetrable. They were speed bumps. But speed bumps work. They slow you down, and in the slowing down there's a chance to choose differently.

There were things I didn't do that, looking back, would have helped. I didn't install website blockers on my laptop; I relied on self-control there and that was a mistake. I didn't give anyone access to my finances to monitor for unusual activity, too embarrassed, even after everything. I didn't call a hotline or see a therapist or join a support group. I handled it alone. It worked, but it was harder than it needed to be. There's no prize for doing this the hard way. If professional help is available to you, use it.

What actually made it work was stacking. No single barrier was enough on its own. The self-exclusion. The deleted apps. The unsaved payment methods. Telling Rose. Telling friends. The meditation thing. The gym. Pouring the energy into work instead of into a phone. Each piece felt small by itself. All of them together meant that getting back to a bet required real, sustained effort across multiple steps instead of one weak moment with a thumb on a screen. That's the only structure I've found that actually beats the urge over time.

Willpower asks you to be strong in the moments when you're weakest. Structure removes the question entirely.

If you're in this right now — still betting, still telling yourself you'll stop on your own. Start with one thing today. Not Monday. Not after one more week. Today. Self-exclude from one app. Delete one platform. Remove one saved card. Tell one person one true thing about what's been happening.

Just one. Then add another. Layer them until the path back to betting is so full of friction that the urge fades before you can act on it.

That's not weakness. That's the only thing that actually works.

CHAPTER 15

Building Something Real

The silence after the crash was louder than I expected.

No notifications. No live odds running in the background. No calculations cycling through my head during games. For four years there had always been something on, some bet running, some outcome pending, some reason to keep one eye on a screen. When that stopped, the quiet had texture. It pressed on things.

The first few weeks were the hardest in a specific way I hadn't anticipated. It wasn't the urges, though those were there. It was the social exposure. Football Sundays with friends, a group of guys watching games together, and within the first ten minutes someone would turn to me — because everyone knew, I was the betting guy in every room I walked into, and ask what I'd taken. Who I liked. What the line was.

I'd say I wasn't betting anymore.

The responses were always some version of the same thing. Disbelief, then a joke, then a shrug and back to the game. Nobody made a big deal of it. But I could feel the slight recalibration happening in real time. The conversation about picks moved to someone else. The group chat about lines that I'd always been part of got quieter for me. Not dramatically. Just gradually, the way things shift when you stop being part of a shared ritual.

I had a friend; I'll call him Tommy — who I'd been texting bets with for years. Tommy bet serious money. Five, ten thousand a unit sometimes, the kind of action that made the games feel like they actually mattered. We'd send each other tickets, celebrate the hits, commiserate the losses. It was its own language, its own form of closeness built around a shared thing we both understood.

When I stopped, me and Tommy stopped talking as much, not because either of us made a decision about it. Just because the main thing that connected our day-to-day conversations was gone. The tough beats that used to bond us had nowhere to land.

While I was writing this book he texted me. He'd missed a parlay to win $250,000 by one leg. I made a joke about starting an anti-gambling course. He laughed and said something about how he needed it, that he kept donating to the casino. It was easy and familiar — the old rhythm coming back for a minute.

But then the conversation ended and we went back to the quiet. Because the joke was the whole conversation. Without the betting there wasn't as much to say, and we both knew it without saying it.

I don't tell that story as a warning about Tommy. He's going to do what he's going to do and that's his life. I tell it because losing that rhythm, the daily texts, the shared language, the identity of being the guys who bet serious money together, was a real cost that I hadn't fully calculated when I decided to stop. The financial math was obvious. The social math was harder.

Some friendships are built on shared values. Some are built on a shared activity. When the activity goes away you find out which kind you had. With Tommy it turned out to be mostly the activity. That isn't a sad ending. It's just what it was, and pretending otherwise wouldn't have changed it.

The thing I had to get honest about — really honest, not just intellectually honest. Was what betting had actually been providing. Because those needs don't disappear when you delete the apps. They just go looking for somewhere else to be met. And if you don't consciously choose what meets them, you'll drift back toward what worked before.

Betting gave me adrenaline. The spike of uncertainty, the physical tension of a game close in the fourth quarter, the release when it went right. That chemical cocktail is real and your body remembers it. The gym replaced some of it, heavy lifting, running, pushing past the point where it's comfortable. The endorphin hit is real and it compounds over time in a way that a bet never does. Better body, clearer head, measurable progress. I started chasing PRs instead of parlays and the progression felt better because it actually built something.

There's a neuroscience reason that swap actually works. The brain's reward circuitry — the dopaminergic pathway that gambling apps target, isn't dedicated to gambling specifically. It's a general-purpose reward system. Anything that produces a measurable, somewhat unpredictable progression; strength gains, business milestones, even a personal record on a run — engages the same circuit. Researchers studying behavioral substitution in addiction recovery have found that the pathway can be functionally re-routed in months, not years, if the new behavior is consistent and offers genuine reward. The gym wasn't replacing betting metaphorically; it was occupying the same neural real estate. That's why it stuck. Distraction doesn't beat the urge. Substitution does.

Betting gave me status. VIP texts from Mike. Courtside seats. The feeling of being sharp when a pick hit, of being the guy who knew things. That validation had gotten woven into how I understood myself. Replacing it meant finding status that was real — business wins, closing deals, hitting targets, team results. Those wins don't evaporate with the next loss. They compound. And there's a specific kind of pride in a win that nobody can take away with a bad beat, because it isn't subject to variance. You earned it. It stays.

Betting gave me escape. When work got stressful or life got heavy, opening the app was an instant way to put everything else on pause.

Problems disappeared for a few hours while I focused on games. Replacing that meant finding escapes that didn't cost money and add stress simultaneously, walks, time with people where phones stayed in pockets, anything that gave my mind genuine rest rather than just redirecting it toward a different kind of anxiety.

And betting gave me social ritual. Talking lines, sharing picks, having money on the game, all of it created a sense of participation, of being inside something that made watching sports feel like more than just watching. That ritual had to be rebuilt around something else. Golf with friends. Pickup basketball. Dinners where I was actually present instead of physically there and mentally somewhere else. The conversations that came out of those were slower to develop than the instant connection of a shared bet, but they ran deeper and they stayed.

Some friendships changed when I stopped. Some quietly faded, like me and Tommy. Others surprised me by getting better once the gambling noise was gone and there was room for something real underneath.

The guys who showed up after I said I was done, who checked in, who asked how I was doing, who didn't make it weird — those friendships became the ones that actually mattered. We rebuilt around dinners and golf and conversations that had nothing to do with lines and spreads. That foundation turned out to be sturdier than anything the betting had built.

I told the people who mattered simply and directly. *I'm done betting. It was consuming too much of my life.* Most were supportive. A few didn't fully get it. That was fine. The point wasn't their understanding; it was saying it out loud to people who knew me, which made going back feel like something more than just breaking a private promise.

The first month without betting was flat in a way I hadn't expected, not painful exactly. Just dull. The intensity I'd been living at. The constant low hum of something on, something to track, something that could go right or wrong at any moment, was gone, and the ordinary pace of days without it felt almost slow by comparison.

I missed the chaos, not the losses, not the shame, not the hiding — just the intensity. The feeling of having something at stake every hour. Life without that felt smaller for a while.

But dull beats anxious. Dull beats checking your phone every five minutes for a score update. Dull beats lying to Rose about where your attention went. Dull beats standing in a hallway at a team event watching a game you don't even care about on your phone because you put money on it at 2pm on a Tuesday.

The flatness didn't last. Over time the new rhythms became the default and I stopped measuring the present against the high of what betting had provided. The business wins started to register as genuinely satisfying rather than just acceptable substitutes. The gym progress became its own form of addiction, measurable, real, mine. The dinners where I was actually present started to feel like the point rather than a consolation prize.

I stopped thinking about what I was missing and started noticing what I was gaining. That shift didn't happen on a schedule. It just happened gradually, the way most real things do; not with a moment of clarity but with a slow accumulation of evidence that something had changed.

The $150,000 taught me what money actually costs when you spend it the wrong way.

Not the dollar amount. The $150,000 is just the number that's easy to say. The real cost was the months of being emotionally unavailable to people who deserved better. The version of myself I became when I was losing. The trust I quietly eroded with Rose by keeping something that significant from her. The dinners I ruined without anyone knowing why. The moments I missed. The attention I gave to a screen instead of to the life that was actually happening in front of me.

The replacements I built aren't as immediately exciting as a parlay hitting. They don't deliver the same spike. What they do is compound. Business revenue growing is slow and steady and real. Strength in the gym is measurable and permanent. Presence with people builds something that doesn't evaporate with a bad beat.

The rush from closing a deal beats any parlay multiplier, not because it's more intense — it isn't. Because it lasts. Because it builds. Because it belongs to you in a way that a bet never does.

That's what I was actually looking for the whole time. I just didn't know it until I stopped looking for it in the wrong place.

CHAPTER 16

Not Ready Yet

If you've made it this far and you're still betting, this chapter is for you.

Not the person who stopped last week, not the person who never had a problem. The person who read everything in this book, recognized themselves in more of it than they wanted to, and still isn't ready to quit. The person who's thinking maybe they can control it better than Julian did. Maybe their situation is a little different. Maybe they just need some guardrails, not a full stop.

I'm not going to argue with you. I was that person too.

About a month after the crash I convinced myself that the problem wasn't betting — it was how I was betting. Too big, too emotional, too reactive. The solution wasn't stopping. It was discipline. I set rules. Smaller stakes. No big parlays. Strict weekly budget. Five hundred dollars max. Singles only. No chasing. No emotional bets. No betting when I was stressed or tired or trying to recover a loss.

It lasted about a week.

A bad beat triggered the old pattern. I was down a few hundred on a game that should have hit, one of those losses that feels less like bad luck and more like a personal insult, like the universe specifically waited for you to put money on something before deciding to go the other way. The frustration built. The voice came back with its familiar logic: *just one recovery bet, get back to even, you were right about the game, the result was a fluke.*

That one recovery bet became another chase. The rules I'd set dissolved so fast it was almost embarrassing in retrospect. Within days I was back to the same patterns, same bet sizes, same emotional decisions, same hiding from Rose, same checking my phone during conversations that deserved my full attention.

The beats kept coming and they kept feeling bigger and more demoralizing, not because the losses were necessarily larger but because each one carried the extra weight of a broken promise. I'd told myself I was done. I'd told myself I was in control. And here I was again, deeper in the same hole, with the added shame of having tried the controlled version and failed at that too.

That month of moderation didn't reduce harm. It prolonged exposure, added more lies, and delayed the only thing that was actually going to work. If you're hiding bets from the people in your life or breaking rules you set for yourself, the moderation phase isn't helping you. It's just giving you a softer story to tell yourself while the damage continues.

I'm telling you that not to make you feel bad about where you are. I'm telling you because I wasted a month finding it out, and you don't have to.

But here's the thing. I also know that some people reading this aren't ready for zero. And telling someone who isn't ready to just stop is about as useful as telling someone who's afraid of heights to just look down. The readiness has to come from somewhere real. You can't manufacture it from the outside.

So if full abstinence feels impossible right now — if zero feels like too far, like a door you can't yet walk through. Here are some things that can slow the bleeding while you build toward it, not because they'll fix the problem. They won't. But because a smaller hole is easier to climb out of than a larger one.

This is a bridge. Not a destination. Don't spend years on the bridge.

The most important financial move you can make right now is separation. Set up a separate account, not your main account, not the one your bills come out of — and transfer a fixed amount into it each month. One to two percent of your disposable income, maximum. When that money is gone, it's gone. No reloading until next month. No credit cards. No loans. No cash advances. No borrowing from friends. No touching savings or emergency funds or money that has a job to do. This creates a ceiling. You can lose the entertainment money. You can't spiral into catastrophic debt if the debt has nowhere to go.

On the bets themselves: skip parlays entirely. We went through the math in Chapter 2. The house keeps roughly half of every dollar you put into a six-leg parlay over time. If you're going to bet, stick to singles. Straight bets have a lower house edge and they don't compound your mistakes the way parlays do. And avoid live betting completely. It's designed for exactly the state you're in when you're chasing, fast, reactive, emotional, no time to think. Every feature of live betting exists to catch you in your worst moment.

Before you place anything, ask yourself three things. Am I chasing a loss right now? If yes, stop. Am I stressed, bored, or emotional? If yes, wait. Can I genuinely afford to lose this amount without it affecting my bills, my savings, or my relationships? If losing it would matter, don't bet it.

The 24-hour rule is simple and it works more often than you'd expect. If you feel the urge to bet, wait 24 hours before acting on it. Most urges don't survive a full day intact. They peak, they look for a way in, and if you don't give them one they fade, not always. But often enough to matter.

Tell someone what you're trying to do. Not the full story necessarily; just that you're trying to bet less, that you're setting limits, that you'd like someone to check in. Even partial accountability is better than none. The secrecy is what lets the problem grow in the dark. Any amount of light helps.

Most apps have deposit limits and timeout features built in. Use them. Set the caps as low as the platform allows. But understand what you're dealing with — apps are designed to nudge you around these protections. They'll send offers. They'll create urgency. They'll make it easy to override your own rules in the moments when your resistance is lowest. Harm reduction is inherently unstable when the other side has more resources dedicated to keeping you betting than you have dedicated to stopping.

Here's what the data says about where you are. In 2025 alone, Americans wagered over $166 billion on sports. Sportsbooks kept nearly $17 billion of that, a record, up over 20% from the year before. About one in three young adults between 21 and 44 placed their first sports bet before they were legally allowed to. Problem-gambling signs show up in roughly 10% of men aged 18 to 30 — double the rate from just a few years ago. Clinical studies on gambling disorder consistently show that controlled gambling has high relapse rates for people with serious problems. The industry knows this. They profit when moderation fails and you come back harder.

I'm not telling you that to scare you. I'm telling you because the thing you're trying to do, moderate, control, manage, is the thing that most people in your position try before they eventually stop. The path you're on has a well-documented trajectory and it doesn't end where you're hoping it ends.

If you've broken your own limits more than once, if you've used credit or moved money you shouldn't have moved to fund bets, if you're hiding what you're doing from people who matter to you, if your mood is tied to whether a bet hits or misses, if betting is affecting your sleep or your work or your relationships, if you think about it more than you think about most other things in your life — harm reduction isn't enough. The problem is deeper than the strategy. You need structural change, not better rules.

I want to be straight with you about something before this chapter ends.

Moderation didn't work for me, not because I didn't try hard enough or want it badly enough. Because I was using a strategy that requires consistent self-regulation against a product specifically engineered to erode self-regulation at exactly the right moment. I was bringing a feeling to a fight that the other side had spent millions of dollars designing. That isn't a fair contest. It was never going to be.

The month I spent trying to control it was a month of smaller losses, more shame, more distance from the people around me, and more evidence that what I actually needed was the thing I was trying to avoid. By the end of it, I wasn't just dealing with the original problem. I was dealing with the original problem plus the failure of the attempt to manage it.

You might need that month. You might need to try the controlled version before you're ready to accept that it doesn't work. That's okay. Most people do. Just don't let one month become six. Don't let the bridge become a place you live.

The goal is zero. Not forever maybe, but for long enough that you can see the pattern clearly, feel what life without it actually feels like, and make a real decision from that place instead of from the middle of the thing you're trying to evaluate.

Cross the bridge. Learn what you need to learn.

Then burn it behind you.

CHAPTER 17

Living Free

Freedom doesn't feel the way I thought it would.

I expected relief. What I got was something quieter. Presence. The ability to be in a room and actually be in it. To sit across from someone and hear what they're saying instead of running calculations in the background of every conversation. To watch a game without money on it and feel the outcome land as something that happened, rather than something that happened to me.

That's what free feels like on a regular Tuesday. Not dramatic. Not cinematic. Just, here. Actually here.

I can have a conversation now without half my mind somewhere else. I can be short-tempered or patient based on what's actually happening in my life rather than whether a bet hit or missed three hours ago. The people around me get the real version instead of the version that was always partially somewhere else, always managing something invisible, always a little colder than the situation called for.

Rose gets the real version now.

I think about what she did and didn't do when I told her about the $45,000. She didn't issue an ultimatum. She didn't make it about herself. She was just worried — quietly, genuinely worried, in the way you get worried about someone when you realize the thing they've been minimizing might be bigger than they're letting on. That worry was enough, not because it scared me into stopping, but because it gave me a reason that existed outside my own head. Someone who mattered could see it. And I didn't want her to keep seeing it.

She's part of why I stopped, not all of it, I had to get there myself, the way you always have to get there yourself. But she was the reason I stopped before it got worse. Before I crossed lines that would have been harder to come back from. I don't know if she fully understands that. I'm not sure I've said it clearly enough.

So I'll say it here. *Rose, you gave me a reason when I needed one. That mattered more than you know.*

I've been back to Atlanta since the crash. Passed through the airport more than once since that Monday afternoon when I sat at the gate and opened Robinhood and saw $0.00.

Every time I walk through that airport I think about that moment, not with the same weight it had then; not the chest tightness, not the hollow replaying of the week, not the shame of a man who had just watched everything disappear and was trying to figure out how to go back to his life like nothing had happened.

I think about it the way you think about a scar. You notice it. You remember how it got there. And then you keep walking.

That version of me sitting at that gate didn't know what came next. Didn't know about Cabo or Matt's words by the fire or the self-exclusion or the three months of distance that slowly became something that felt like solid ground. Didn't know that the same airport would become just an airport again someday — a place you pass through on the way to somewhere else rather than a monument to the worst week of your life.

It's just an airport now. That feels like progress.

I won't tell you the urges are gone. They're not. They cycle through on schedule — paycheck days especially, when the money hits and the old voice surfaces with its familiar logic. Big games. Moments when friends around me are talking about their bets and not betting feels like opting out of something. Stressful stretches when the escape hatch the apps used to provide would feel useful if I let myself think about it that way.

What I'm describing without using the clinical name for it is something called *inhibitory learning*, a framework developed by clinical psychologist Michelle Craske at UCLA. The old understanding of cravings was that they extinguished, got smaller and smaller until they disappeared. Newer research suggests that's wrong. The original urge pattern doesn't get erased; instead, the brain builds a competing learned response on top of it. Each time you feel an urge and don't act on it, the new pathway gets stronger relative to the old one. The urges themselves stay roughly constant in intensity. What changes is your brain's ability to ride them out without giving them the action they used to demand. That matches my experience exactly. I'm not someone who feels less pull. I'm someone who has stopped mistaking the pull for a command.

I don't act on them, not because I've become someone who doesn't feel them, but because I've become someone who knows what they are. A feeling. A wave. Something that rises and passes if you don't feed it. I'm stronger than the urge now, not because the urge got weaker but because I stopped mistaking it for a command.

And I know what's on the other side of acting on it, not the theoretical consequence but the specific one — the Atlanta airport, the $0.00, the flight home where I stared at a Netflix show I don't remember and didn't sleep and sat with the wreckage of a week that didn't have to happen.

I won't risk money I have for money I don't need. Not again. That sentence. The one Matt said by the fire in Cabo without knowing he was saying it about me, became the clearest definition I have of what I was doing for five years. *Chasing money I didn't need. Losing money I already had.* I don't need to keep learning that lesson.

I've partially recovered the money. Not all of it. Some. The slow grinding way — work, saving, investing, building revenue streams that compound instead of evaporating. The bank statements are boring now. That's on purpose. Boring means stable. Boring means what's there stays there.

My mom still doesn't know. She worked two jobs for years so I could have the kind of life where losing $150,000 in a week was even possible, and she'll never know it happened. I carry that quietly, not as shame exactly, more as a reminder of what money actually represents when you understand where it came from and what it cost someone to help you get to a place where you could earn it.

The $150,000 is gone. What it bought me; the pattern recognition, the clarity, the understanding of exactly how these systems work and exactly how my own brain responds to them — that's mine in a way the money never fully was. You can't take away what you learned from losing it.

If you're reading this at 2am with the app open and a bet half-built and the familiar voice telling you this one is different — I was you. Exactly you. Sitting in the dark convincing myself the next one would fix what the last one broke.

It won't. Not because you're weak or stupid or uniquely prone to this. Because the math doesn't care who you are, and the system was built by people whose job was to make sure you never fully believed that until it was too late.

You don't have to learn it the $150,000 way.

Tell one person something true tonight. Delete one app before you go to sleep. Make one decision that your future self will thank you for even if your present self resents it.

The life on the other side of this, the one where you're actually present in your own conversations, where your mood belongs to you instead of to a scoreboard, where the people who love you get the real version of who you are, that life is waiting. It doesn't require perfection. It doesn't require never feeling the pull again. It just requires not acting on it.

One choice at a time.

The last bet is the one you don't place.

CHAPTER 18

Three Things I Haven't Said Out Loud

I wrote these and didn't send them. Some are versions of conversations I might still have. Some are conversations I never will. They're here because part of what gambling did was put words in my mouth that weren't true, and part of what stopping has been is figuring out which of the unspoken true ones I want to send back into the world.

To Rose

I never told you about all of it.

I told you about the $45,000 because it had become impossible not to. I dressed it up as a bad beat because I was scared of how the bigger truth would land between us. The bigger truth was four years long. The bigger truth had a $150,000 number at the end of it. The bigger truth was that for a long stretch of our relationship I was somewhere else mentally even when I was right next to you, and you noticed, and you didn't make me explain it because you were waiting for me to get there on my own.

You didn't have to do that. You did it anyway. I think about that a lot.

The dinner with your parents. I don't know if you ever knew what I was actually doing under the table. I don't know if you suspected and chose not to ask, or if you genuinely thought I was being polite-but-distracted in the way people sometimes are at meet-the-parents dinners. Either way, I owed your parents a different version of me that night, and I owed you a version of me that was actually paying attention to what you'd built up to introducing them to. I gave them and you a worse version. I'm sorry for that more than I've said.

You gave me a reason to stop before I knew I needed one. I don't know if you understood that's what you were doing. I'm telling you now in case you didn't.

To Mom

You worked two jobs for me. I don't say that to be sentimental. I say it because I need you to know I never forgot it, even during the years I was doing a very good job pretending I had.

You don't know what happened. I've decided not to tell you. I've gone back and forth on that more than once. The argument for telling you is that you raised me to face hard things directly, and I'm not doing that here. The argument for not telling you is that knowing wouldn't undo any of it, and the only thing the knowledge would do is move some weight from me to you, and you've already carried enough.

If you ever read this book and figure out it was me, I want you to know that the lessons stuck. The version of me you raised is still in here. He just took a longer route than he should have. He's back now.

The money that's gone is gone. The thing that wasn't gone, the thing nothing could touch, was the discipline you built into me before I knew what to call it. That came back. It's what got me out.

I love you. I don't say that the way you taught me to. I'm trying to.

To Tom

I don't know what to say to you that I haven't already failed to say in person.

I sent you money. I should have sent you my time. The money was easier. The money let me feel like I was helping while keeping the actual hard thing, sitting with you, asking real questions, not letting you change the subject, at arm's length. You needed someone to not let you change the subject. I changed it with you, every time, because I was scared of where it would go if we stayed there.

I don't know where you are right now. I think about you. I want you to know that even on the days when I don't reach out, I think about you.

If you ever read this and recognize yourself in it, the door I walked through is still open. It isn't a clean door. It doesn't make any of the harder parts easier. But it goes somewhere. I came through it and the room on the other side has light in it.

I'd sit with you on either side of that door for as long as you needed.

I should have said that already.

I'm saying it now.

Author's Note

This book was written under a pseudonym to protect my privacy and the privacy of those in my life. The events, amounts, and timeline are true. Some names and identifying details have been changed.

If you or someone you know is struggling with gambling, please reach out. Recovery is possible. You're not alone.

1-800-GAMBLER, free, confidential support, available 24/7

National Council on Problem Gambling, ncpgambling.org

Self-exclusion programs in your state, searchable at ncpgambling.org

You can reach out anonymously. You can get help without shame.

— Julian Harlow

A Note on Sources

The statistics, research findings, and case studies referenced throughout this book are drawn from a combination of industry reports, academic research, and reputable journalistic sources. In some cases, details have been paraphrased or contextualized for narrative clarity, but all figures and claims are grounded in publicly available data or documented reporting.

Industry Statistics

Global sports betting market size (2024)

Grand View Research, Global Sports Betting Market Size & Share Report, 2024.

Estimated global market value of approximately $100.9 billion.

U.S. Sports betting revenue and post-2018 expansion

American Gaming Association, State of the States: The AGA Survey of the Commercial Casino Industry, 2024.

U.S. Sports betting revenue reached a record $13.71 billion following continued expansion after the 2018 Supreme Court decision.

U.S. Sports wagering handle and revenue (2025)

American Gaming Association, press release, February 26, 2026.

Americans wagered $166.94 billion on sports in 2025; sportsbooks generated $16.96 billion in revenue, a 22.8% increase over 2024.

Growth in gambling-related help-seeking behavior following legalization

Yeola, Allen, Desai, Poliak, Yang, Smith, and Ayers,

"Growing Health Concern Regarding Gambling Addiction in the Age of Sportsbooks,"

JAMA Internal Medicine, April 2025.

Study found retail sportsbook openings led to a 33% increase in gambling addiction-related search activity, with online sportsbook launches producing a sustained 61% increase.

Youth and Problem Gambling

Early exposure to sports betting among young adults

National Council on Problem Gambling (NCPG), Harris Poll Survey, 2026.

Approximately 33% of adults aged 21--44 reported placing a sports bet before the legal age of 21.

Problem gambling prevalence among young men

Fairleigh Dickinson University Poll, 2024.

Roughly 10% of men aged 18--30 exhibited behaviors consistent with problem gambling, compared to approximately 3% of the general population.

Suicidal ideation among problem gamblers

UK Gambling Commission, public health data and analysis.

Studies indicate that approximately one in five problem gamblers report experiencing suicidal thoughts within a given year.

Behavioral and Psychological Research

Concepts related to dopamine, intermittent reinforcement, and habit formation are based on widely accepted findings in neuroscience and behavioral psychology, including research on reward systems, addiction pathways, and decision-making under uncertainty.

These ideas are synthesized from established academic literature and public-facing summaries from organizations including the American Psychiatric Association and the National Institute on Drug Abuse.

Case Studies and Reporting

Archie Karas ("The Run")

Documented accounts from casino history archives and multiple published reports describing one of the largest winning and losing streaks in Las Vegas history.

Phil Mickelson gambling losses

Reported in Gambler: Secrets from a Life at Risk (2023) by Billy Walters, along with interviews and public statements by Mickelson acknowledging gambling-related issues.

Loss estimates and betting activity are based on reported claims and should be understood in that context.

Lottery winner case studies

Historical reporting on lottery winners who later lost significant wealth, including widely documented examples such as Evelyn Adams, who won multiple jackpots and later lost the majority of her winnings through gambling.

Massachusetts gambling trends following legalization

WBUR News investigative reporting, 2025.

Findings indicated a significant increase in gambling-related referrals and help-seeking behavior, particularly among younger demographics, following the launch of legal sports betting.

Behavioral Economics and Decision Research

House-money effect and mental accounting

Richard H. Thaler and Eric J. Johnson, "Gambling with the House Money and Trying to Break Even: The Effects of Prior Outcomes on Risky Choice," *Management Science*, June 1990.
Richard H. Thaler, "Mental Accounting and Consumer Choice," *Marketing Science*, 1985.
Thaler's research demonstrates that decision-makers treat recent winnings as psychologically separate from their original stake, increasing willingness to take risks with the winnings. Thaler received the Nobel Memorial Prize in Economic Sciences in 2017 for related contributions to behavioral economics.

Loss aversion and prospect theory

Daniel Kahneman and Amos Tversky, "Prospect Theory: An Analysis of Decision under Risk," *Econometrica*, March 1979.
Foundational work establishing that losses are weighted approximately twice as heavily as equivalent gains in human decision-making. Kahneman received the Nobel Memorial Prize in Economic Sciences in 2002 for this body of work.

Clinical and Psychological Research

Impact on partners of problem gamblers

Reviews and primary studies in the *Journal of Gambling Studies* and *Addiction*, 2010s–2020s.
A consistent body of research finds elevated rates of depression, anxiety, chronic stress, and concealment-related cognitive load

among the cohabiting partners of individuals with gambling disorder, with effects often persisting after the disordered gambling itself stops.

Attention residue and task-switching costs

Sophie Leroy, "Why Is It So Hard to Do My Work? The Challenge of Attention Residue When Switching Between Work Tasks," *Organizational Behavior and Human Decision Processes*, 2009.
Research demonstrating that incomplete switches between tasks impose measurable cognitive costs on subsequent performance, with attention partially remaining on the unresolved prior task.

The knowing–doing gap

Jeffrey Pfeffer and Robert I. Sutton, *The Knowing-Doing Gap: How Smart Companies Turn Knowledge into Action* (Harvard Business School Press, 2000).
A widely cited treatment of the persistent gap between knowing what should be done and acting on that knowledge, with parallels in clinical research on early-stage addiction recovery.

Behavioral substitution and reward pathways in recovery

Reviews on neuroplasticity and reward-system substitution from the National Institute on Drug Abuse and the American Society of Addiction Medicine.
Findings consistent with the view that the brain's general-purpose reward circuitry can be re-engaged by alternative behaviors offering genuine, somewhat variable reward, with measurable changes in functional response over months of consistent practice.

Inhibitory learning and exposure-based recovery

Michelle G. Craske et al., "Maximizing Exposure Therapy: An Inhibitory Learning Approach," *Behaviour Research and Therapy*, 2014.

Inhibitory learning theory holds that exposure-based interventions do not erase original fear or craving learning; rather, they produce competing learned associations that, with practice, dominate the response to the original cue. The framework has been influential in modern treatment of anxiety disorders and is increasingly applied to behavioral addictions.

Final Note

This book is not intended as a statistical or academic text, but as a synthesis of personal experience, publicly available data, and documented patterns observed across individuals and systems. The goal is clarity, not technical exhaustiveness.

Where exact figures are cited, they reflect the most recent available data at the time of writing. Where broader patterns are described, they are supported by multiple sources and consistent findings across research and reporting.

www.ingramcontent.com/pod-product-compliance
Lightning Source LLC
LaVergne TN
LVHW010840120826
845149LV00017B/3336

* 9 7 9 8 9 9 5 7 2 8 2 0 7 *